TAKE THE TRAIN FROM HITCHIN

TAKE THE TRAIN FROM HITCHIN

A Journey Into Our
Local Railway Heritage

by
Phil Howard

To Stuart,
Happy 70th.
Phil Howard
14/10/06

A Hitchin Historical Society Publication

A Hitchin Historical Society Publication 2006

ISBN 0-9552411-0-3
978-0-9552411-0-9

Design, reprographics and print by
Digital Imagin, Letchworth, Hertfordshire. Telephone 01462 678154

Cover photograph:	A4 pacific 60029 "Woodcock" leaving Hitchin with the 0820 Kings Cross-Doncaster train on 27 January 1959, on a very atmospheric cold winter's morning (Michael Joyce collection)
Inside front cover:	1923 OS 25" map showing the southern approaches to Hitchin station
Half title page:	Replica British Railways Hitchin station 'totem'
Frontispiece:	A view from the 1970s looking north from Hitchin Yard Box: note the semaphore signals and the pleasing absence of overhead line equipment. A wagon is being unloaded in the goods shed and a Baby Deltic waits in the up siding. In the centre distance the Cambridge Junction Box is just visible. (Roy Revell Collection)
Inside back cover:	1922 OS 25" map showing the northern approaches to Hitchin station.

TIMETABLE

DEDICATION
This book is dedicated to the memory of two
Hitchin train drivers, both of whom I knew
well, and who passed away at an early age
through illness:
Kevin Sharp in 1995 and David Lawson in 2001

ACKNOWLEDGEMENTS

The publication of this book would not have been possible without the assistance and patience from the people below:

Members of the Hitchin Historical Society, particularly Scilla Douglas, Zena Grant, David Howlett, Pauline Humphries, Simon Walker and Derek Wheeler.

Special thanks to Phil Rowe of the society for his railway knowledge and many evenings of research through mounds of paperwork and photographs.

Hitchin railwaymen, serving and retired: Peter Newberry, John Toddington, Dave Preston, Vaughan Bloom, Roy Revell and George Howe.

Also contributions from Len Springett, Derek Talbot, Allan Sibley, Vivienne Kent, Neil Bethell, David Percival, John Scorer, Colin Barlow, Derrick Else, Bob Wheeler, Peter Waylett, Roy Woods, Steve Pearce, Ivor Walton, John Rogers, Keith Wilson, Jim Bowskill, Keith & Irene Hopkins, David Lawrence, Basil Coles; and the following contributors who are sadly no longer with us: Neil Alston, Michael Joyce and Tony Chambers.

Gill Riding, David Hodges, and the staff at Hitchin Museum.

Caroline Frith for her line drawings of original station features.

Steve Rogers and staff at the Corn Exchange, Hitchin, for use of their premises and assistance with the Book Launch.

Barrie Dack and Chris Murray at Digital Imagin must be congratulated for their production skills.

The staff at Hitchin Station.

Also thanks to my father Ivan, now in his 80th year, for taking me train spotting at an early age which I'm sure sparked my interest in railways.

Special thanks to my wife Chris for her patience in assisting me in hours of research and to my daughter Julie for her typing and computer skills.

Phil Howard, September 2006.

INTRODUCTION

My interest in railways started as a trainspotter in and around Hitchin in the 1950s and '60s. This interest continued when I left school in 1965, joining the railway at Hitchin. For five years I was a 'secondman' on diesel locomotives, leaving in 1970 to fulfil another boyhood dream: to become a firefighter, a career from which I retired in 2004.

Having a large collection of railway books, it occurred to me that a book about the railway at Hitchin was overdue. The potential content is enormous, for example: Hitchin had two steam sheds, then a diesel shed, a branch line to Bedford, branch line to Cambridge and a permanent way engineer's yard. The book aims to give the reader a personal insight into the railway at Hitchin, from its construction to the present day. It is hoped also that it combines the interest of both railway enthusiast and those with a fascination for local history.

Phil Howard, September 2006.

HItchin Station, photographed from the Yard Box, in the early 1970s, on a quiet summer Sunday afternoon. Loaded luggage trolleys wait on the up platform, the water tank looms in the centre, and Benslow Bridge is just visible in the distance. (Roy Revell collection)

FOREWORD

Hitchin's place in Hertfordshire's local history is firmly rooted in the fact that it is one of the longest continually inhabited towns in the county and, from early medieval times, was a key religious, administrative, market and service centre. Such importance was, however, not maintained without responding to change, and this was especially true once the agricultural and industrial developments of the eighteenth century accelerated. It followed that one of the most important events in the town's modern history was the coming, between 1850 and 1857, of two major railway lines - the Great Northern and the Midland. Through these Hitchin was connected to much wider sources of influence, confronted with both opportunities and threats and pushed into an increased tempo of life that has not diminished since.

Since the nineteenth century, then, railways have been a key part of Hitchin's town life. In 1815 local postmaster and historian William Dunnage wrote that a railway link to navigable water to the north might help counter Ware's river-borne threat to our local malt trade. And this vision predated by almost a decade the beginnings of the railway age proper, with the opening of the Stockton and Darlington and Liverpool and Manchester railways in 1825 and 1830. After 1850 the railway became - and remains - central to Hitchin's well being. Initially that central role was dominated by corn and coal, later by consumer items such as fish, ice and visiting circuses, and today it is fulfilled by commuters.

It is a very great pleasure to recommend Phil Howard's fascinating book on Hitchin's railways. His personal account brings many aspects of our town's railway history vividly to life. It reminds us that the railway scene itself is constantly changing and what people of Phil's and my generation looked on as everyday things have already taken on the character of historical curiosity and are worthy of record for future generations. It is also a great pleasure to recognise Phil's book as another valuable contribution to Hitchin's wider local history prepared with the help of the Hitchin Historical Society's indefatigable publications team. And, on cue, it is appropriate that it will appear just as we are about to celebrate in 2007 the 150th anniversary of the coming of the Midland Railway to Hitchin.

David Howlett
Chairman, Hitchin Historical Society
1992-1996

Hitchin,
September 2006

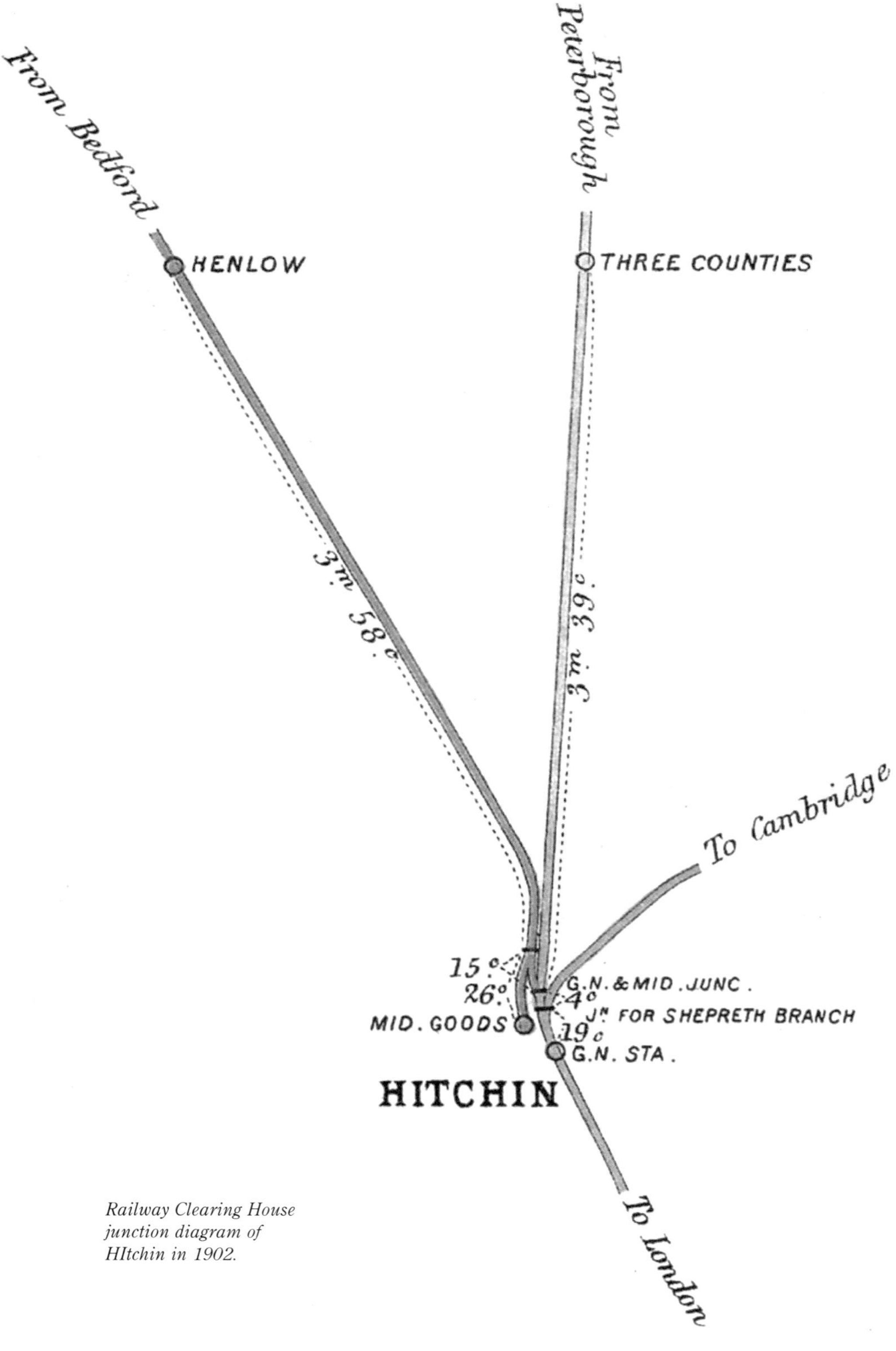

From Bedford

From Peterborough

HENLOW

THREE COUNTIES

3 ᵐ 58 ᶜ

3 ᵐ 33 ᶜ

To Cambridge

15°

26°

4°

MID. GOODS

G.N.& MID.JUNC.

Jⁿ FOR SHEPRETH BRANCH

19°

G.N. STA.

HITCHIN

To London

Railway Clearing House junction diagram of HItchin in 1902.

THE EARLY YEARS

R ailway fever caught on in the 1830 – 1840 period as many railway bills were brought before Parliament for its approval. Not many of these succeeded but a Parliamentary notice appeared in "The Times" newspaper on 17 April 1844 announcing the proposed London to York line, which was to run through Hitchin.

As Hitchin was to be a station along the proposed route, a meeting was called to summon the inhabitants of Hitchin and the surrounding area to meet at the Sun Hotel in Hitchin at 3pm on 8 June 1844. There, the following resolution was passed:

> "That in the opinion of this meeting a Railway furnishing the most direct communication with London and the manufacturing and coal districts having a station at Hitchin would offer many advantages to the Town and Neighbourhood and deserves of the support of the inhabitants."

A poster advertising a public meeting at the Sun Hotel about the proposed railway through Hitchin (Hitchin Museum)

It was obvious that the strength of feeling from the populace of Hitchin and the surrounding area that support for the railway was very great, the reasons being made very clear.

When the 1845 session of Parliament opened there were no fewer than 224 railway bills awaiting approval.

There was considerable debate before the London to York bill received Royal Assent on 26 July 1846. A month later the company, now reformed as the Great Northern Railway, held its first general meeting.

The line northwards out of London was surveyed and work began towards the end of 1846. Mr Joseph Cubitt was appointed Engineer in Chief and Mr Thomas Brassey the contractor. The task of these two early pioneers was to be no mean feat.

The line from London to York entailed laying 328 miles of track. Cubitt's plans involved the removal of some fourteen and a half million cubic yards of earthwork, the building of fourteen tunnels and about 420 bridges. The most ambitious construction was that of the Welwyn viaduct which was needed to carry the line over the River Mimram valley. This structure was to be 1560 feet long and 98 feet high, needing forty 30 foot arches to span the valley. Work on the viaduct was delayed for some weeks in the winter of 1849 – 1850 by very severe frosts.

As construction of the line moved slowly north out of London the next major challenge to the contractors after Welwyn viaduct was the laying of the line through Hitchin, which brought its own problems. Not only were there issues of land ownership to be resolved, there was the challenge to overcome a large hill of chalk where the route was planned.

THE LINE THROUGH HITCHIN

The route of the railway through Hitchin was not easy, and soon encountered a few problems. Ideally it should have passed through the centre of the town, but Lord Dacre objected, saying it would be too close to his park.

Hitchin historian Reginald Hine was of the opinion that it was the Delmé-Radcliffe family of Hitchin Priory who objected, and they also had a park to protect; hence the station is one mile from the town centre as we know it today.

For the line to come through Hitchin, a deep cutting needed to be made through Benslow Hill.

The chalk debris from the cutting was dumped on the northern side of Hitchin to form an embankment (locally known as Lime Bank) which would carry the railway from Grove Mill meadows northwards towards Arlesey. In a contemporary account of the excavation found in Hitchin Museum, we read that "the London and York Railway by 7 August 1848 had 957 men and 193 horses at work in the Hitchin district."

In July 1850 Hitchin station was opened.

It was a simple building built on open fields between Hitchin and Walsworth. It

A picture, said to be of the line under construction near Benslow, Hitchin, in 1848. (Hitchin Museum)

Hitchin station in 1866 with 'The Alps' footbridge spanning the tracks. Locomotive No 53, standing at the 'up' platform, was built by Hawthorn of Newcastle. Benslow Bridge can be seen in the distance. (A Latchmore photograph, Hitchin Museum)

had no cover over the booking hall entrance or the platforms. Passengers had to cross the tracks to reach the London-bound up platform. (In railway terms, generally "up" means towards London and "down" means away from London.) A stationmaster's cottage was built on the up platform and, because of the obvious danger of passengers crossing the tracks, a footbridge was built across the lines to connect the platforms. This footbridge became affectionately known locally as the "Alps". The priority of the contractors was to keep forging northwards with the construction of the line, and no real improvements were made to the station until 1911.

READY FOR THE FIRST TRAIN

Once the construction of the line had progressed beyond Peterborough the stage was set for the first train to run to Hitchin and on to Peterborough. The train left Maiden Lane station just north of King's Cross at 9am on Monday 5 August 1850.

The train consisted of seventeen carriages. Some were elegantly-furnished first class carriages. Plainer second and third class teak-panelled carriages formed most of the train, shining with coats of new varnish. As the train made its way out of the suburbs of north London it passed through East Barnet and then Potters Bar, where more passengers joined it.

Even though these stations were unfinished, they were garlanded with evergreens and flowers and lined with spectators. As the train passed some halts, guns were fired in salute to this novel means of transport.

By now the train had entered Hertfordshire and arrived at Hatfield.

The passengers could see Hatfield House and the town from the station. The train departed from Hatfield to the cheers of a large crowd at 10am, and soon reached the splendid Welwyn viaduct where it stopped in the centre.

Some of the travellers alighted to admire the viaduct and the views of the Mimram valley below.

The viaduct was almost 100 feet above the river and constructed of forty semi-circular arches. Sixteen million bricks went into the construction, and Hexham stone was brought from the north for copings and arches. The Great Northern Railway company must have been proud of its engineering achievement.

The passengers reoccupied their seats and the train continued to Welwyn station and on through Digswell tunnel and through yet another tunnel under Woolmer Green Wood. The next landmark passed was Knebworth House.

Perhaps it was a coincidence that Lord Lytton of Knebworth House had chosen this particular day to entertain many of the local people. His dislike of the railway near his country home was intense.

When plans for a new station at Broadwater were proposed, he was horrified. However by 1886 timber from the Knebworth estate was being sold to the Great Northern Railway which indicated that he had overcome his prejudice by this time.

As the train continued on its way towards Stevenage the very first major rail accident nearly occurred! The coupling chain between the ninth and tenth carriages snapped and the last eight vehicles were left behind.

The forward section of the train continued on its journey at ever increasing speed. The driver was unaware he was deserting a large number of his passengers until he was alerted by a passing ballast train, travelling in the opposite direction. The engine was reversed and the stray carriages were once more linked to the back of the train, much to the relief of concerned passengers.

The train now proceeded on its way towards Hitchin. It passed over the girder bridge still in use in 1973 at Little Wymondley, and through the Benslow Hill cutting to Hitchin station. At this time it was sometimes known as Walsworth station as it lay just outside that hamlet.

At the station the train stopped and the passengers were welcomed by crowds of ladies and gentlemen who waved their handkerchiefs and cheered enthusiastically, both on the arrival and departure of the train.

The railway company proposed that Hitchin should be a "first class" as well as a working station where locomotives would be serviced and stored. Hitchin was now well and truly on the railway map. The train set off once more crossing the River Hiz over a four arched bridge and recrossing the river again in Walsworth. A twenty-foot girder bridge had been erected over the spring at Cadwell where the line continued into Bedfordshire.

PETERBOROUGH AT LAST!

The train steamed into Peterborough station at twenty minutes to two; nearly four and a half hours after it had left London!

The platforms at Peterborough were splendidly decorated and many tables of refreshments were provided for the passengers before their return journey to London. Many speeches were made and toasts drunk, including one to the contractor for the line, Thomas Brassey, who provided the refreshments.

Also toasted were Joseph Cubitt, Engineer in Chief of the line, without whose skills the project would not have succeeded, and Mr A Ransome of Ipswich, who had employed over a thousand navvies on the construction of the line.

Hence the railway through Hitchin had seen its first train, with regular passenger trains commencing three days later.

HITCHIN WELCOMES QUEEN VICTORIA

The following year, the directors of the Great Northern were delighted to hear that Queen Victoria would travel by their railway as far as Doncaster on her annual visit to Balmoral Castle.

It was not the first time the Queen had travelled by rail but the first time the Great Northern was honoured by her patronage.

The royal party left Buckingham Palace at half past one on 27 August 1851. The Queen departed in the royal train from Maiden Lane at two o'clock and travelled at about thirty miles an hour. The train reached Hitchin station about ten past three.

The first task on arrival was to fill the engine with water. The station was decorated with flags, evergreens and flowers, and lined with men, women and children. The clergymen of the district were present, and soldiers lined the platform to prevent the excited crowd from pushing too near the train.

One young lady in the crowd, a Miss Exton, was fortunate that the Queen's compartment stopped opposite her on the platform. Prince Albert and the Queen stood up and moved to the window, acknowledging the cheers of the crowd. Miss Exton moved forward and presented Her Majesty with a beautiful arrangement of flowers which were graciously accepted. After a few minutes the train moved off to the sound of the people singing "God save the Queen", led by a large choir of school children. The Queen had not visited this part of the country before, and all those who could be there lined the track for several miles out of Hitchin to watch the Royal progress to the north. Farm labourers, old squires on horseback and school children from miles around went to see Queen Victoria for the first time.

TWO

THE MIDLAND
COMES TO HITCHIN

Now that Hitchin had received the royal seal of approval, it was soon to see more visitors in the form of passengers of the Midland Railway. In the railway mania that existed at the time the main aim of companies was to build a line to London to capture the lucrative passenger and goods market that the capital inevitably provided.

In 1847 the Midland made its first application to Parliament to build a line from Leicester (Wigston) to Bedford, with an extension to Hitchin.

Although permission was obtained, the application eventually lapsed due to lack of finance.

In August 1853 the Midland was persuaded to apply again to build the line from Leicester to Hitchin. This time, the impetus came from iron ore companies in Northamptonshire and a deputation of land owners in Bedfordshire, William Henry Whitbread being one of the most prominent. Again permission was granted. The company surveyor, Charles Liddell, estimated that it would cost £304,000 to build the Hitchin to Bedford extension and a further £596,000 from Bedford to Leicester at £19,000 per mile.

The Midland found difficulty in raising the capital for the project at the time due to the struggling economy and the threat of war in the Crimea. Because of the need to keep expensive structures such as viaducts and tunnels to a minimum, the gradient profile of the line was severe: as much as 1 in 120 in places, quite steep in railway terms.

An example was a stiff climb of 1 in 132 from Cardington station up to Warden tunnel near Southill. Thomas Brassey was appointed as construction engineer, once again building a line to Hitchin. Work began on the construction of the line in autumn 1853.

The first village along the line was Ickleford. A long embankment was built at this point, with bridges taking the line over the old Icknield Way and Arlesey Road. Material for the construction of part of the embankment was dug from two "borrows". This left two long, deep, narrow pits adjacent to the bridge that crossed the Icknield Way. These pits soon flooded.

The feature became known as Gerry's Hole. Legend has it that Gerry – a local character – drowned in the pool after a long session in the pub. Another (certainly untrue) rumour had it that the area was named after "Jerry", a Messerschmitt pilot, whose plane was said to have crashed here during the Second World War.

Today, the pit is a wildlife conservation area, attracting many species of birds, insects and other forms of flora and fauna.

In 1945, Ickleford applied to the London Midland & Scottish Railway (successor to the Midland) to have a halt built, as many of the villagers worked in Hitchin, Stevenage or London. This was to be a small station, with trains stopping by request only. The proposal was unsuccessful, as the railway company was not convinced there would be enough demand for a station at this location.

SLOWLY BUT SURELY THE LINE IS BUILT

The building of the line progressed slowly over the first year due to lack of manpower. In mid 1854 there were several military campaigns in progress and labourers preferred to serve their country rather than work long hours on the railway or labouring in the fields.

There were several villages along the route of the line and, with a large number of navvies employed, these quiet villages had their peace disturbed to a great extent. In July 1854 the Midland employed several scripture readers at 200 guineas per year in an attempt to quieten the workmen down.

There were no public houses in the vicinity of the line so an ordinary house in the hamlet of Ireland between Cardington and Shefford was converted into a public house and named the "Black Horse", which was only a few yards from the line, and is still with us today.

The most extensive work on the line was the half-mile Warden tunnel between Cardington and Southill, constructed by local builder John Knowles of Shefford. Now part of a nature reserve, it is still there, but inaccessible.

Bricks for the tunnel were made at a brickyard in Old Warden but, yet again, manpower proved to be a problem.

In the summers of 1855 and 1856 many labourers, who were local men, left to work in the fields and help gather in the harvest. This exodus to the fields reduced the work force by a quarter.

There was a danger that the construction of the line would not be completed in time, and the company sought more productivity and longer hours, the tunnel being completed in late 1856.

Unfortunately as sometimes happened in major construction work in this era, there were several accidents in the vicinity of Southill. In February 1855 some labourers were excavating a cutting when part of it collapsed burying two men.

One of them died before he could be released; the other, a 23-year-old labourer named Trust King, was dug out alive but his injuries were severe and he died a few hours later.

Shortly afterwards at the north end of Warden tunnel as earth was being loaded into wagons the embankment collapsed burying a labourer named Charles Clarke. He was quickly dug out by his fellow labourers but died shortly afterwards.

A lad of only 15 years of age named John Thompson was working in the brickyard at Old Warden helping to make bricks for the tunnel, the poor lad lost an arm when he caught it in a clay grinding machine.

Stations at Henlow, Shefford, Southill and Cardington were built in 1856 (described in more detail later in this chapter) mainly with bricks from the Old Warden brickworks.

As the line was to be a main line to Hitchin double track was laid for its entire length. The Midland became involved in a dispute with the Great Northern Railway over half an acre of land that they needed for a junction near Arlesey, so that they could join the Main Line.

This was not resolved so the line had to run parallel for some way, to join at a junction at Hitchin.

THE FIRST TRAIN RUNS

The line from Leicester to Bedford, then to Hitchin, was completed on 8 April 1857. The first trains over the line were goods trains. An inspection of the line was undertaken by company directors and H.M. Inspector of Railways and it was opened to passenger traffic on 7 May.

The first train to Bedford left Hitchin at 7.33am on this date, consisting of 18 carriages, and arrived at Bedford at 8.15am, some 3,000 tickets being sold.

Such was the excitement of the first train arriving from Hitchin that the Mayor declared a gala day and many shops and factories closed to allow people to go along and celebrate at the station.

The opening of the line had an immediate effect on farms and smallholdings along the line. They could now send their agricultural produce and livestock to an ever-demanding market in London. Each station had sheep and cattle pens, and of course a coal yard. Cheap coal became the norm, and villagers came from miles around to buy it.

In 1858 there were 5 passenger trains per day in each direction. Morning trains were full of commuters and school children, the journey taking 20 minutes to Shefford and 40 minutes to Bedford.

Market days in Hitchin and Bedford were very important to the local and rural community. Many people travelled to and fro between the market towns just to visit another market. The journey by road could take many hours so the trip by train lasting only 40 minutes became so popular that an extra train was provided to cater for the demand.

The remains of the Midland goods sheds, following the 1891 gale.
(Hitchin Museum)

The Midland engine shed in Nightingale Road, with the diesel depot on the right.
The foreground is the site of Bowman's Mill, replaced by a B&Q store built in 1985.
(Neil Alston collection)

*A view of Midland Cottages, flanked by the Midland railway embankment,
in 1995, looking north from Ransom's Recreation Ground (Scilla Douglas)*

THE MIDLAND SETTLES AT HITCHIN

The Midland tried to be as independent as possible at Hitchin. Two engine sheds were built, both with two bays for storing locomotive spare parts and undertaking minor repairs on the locomotives. These were to the west of the main line and covered a considerable area. A 42ft locomotive turntable was built adjacent to the sheds, having been transferred from Bedford in 1894. This allowed locomotives to be turned so that they could run forward to Bedford. Disaster struck one of these sheds in November 1891 when a severe gale blew down most of the shed leaving only the gable end standing.

There were a considerable number of Midland staff working at the depot and, to accommodate them, a row of cottages was built at the bottom of the embankment adjacent to the yard. These cottages were aptly named "Midland Cottages" and are still occupied today, although considerable modernisation has taken place over the years.

A large Midland goods shed was constructed next to the engine sheds, and Nightingale Road became very busy with horse-drawn wagons conveying goods and luggage between the station and various locations throughout the town.

Weary travellers arriving at Hitchin from Leicester and the North could take refreshment at the Leicester Railway Inn (now The Nightingale) in Nightingale Road and the more wealthy could buy accommodation for the night.

STATIONS ALONG THE LINE (HITCHIN TO BEDFORD)

Henlow station, in the late 1950s, looking towards Shefford. Note the crossing gates closed at the end of the platform, ready for a passing train. (David Lawrence collection)

HENLOW

Henlow station was built in 1856 in a style unique to the Hitchin and Leicester railway. It had ornamental diamond paned windows, as was the case with some other stations along the line. The station served the population of Henlow and surrounding villages. It came into its own in 1917 when Henlow Camp was established, becoming a repair depot the following year. Goods sidings were built and standard gauge track was laid across the road to link the sidings with other parts of the camp.

The camp itself was served by its own internal 2 foot gauge 'decauville' narrow gauge railway system. The decauville system was an "off-the-shelf" system of narrow-gauge railways, used in industrial or agricultural situations when there was a relatively temporary need, or where the layout of the rails needed to be changed from time to time. Invented by Paul Decauville (1846-1922) a French engineer, the track resembled a giant's toy railway. The Decauville factory produced track, wagons and locomotives. Like "Hoover" to the vacuum cleaner, decauville railways came to be the generic term for any railway of this kind.

Henlow's internal narrow-gauge system was constructed in the 1920s and was primarily used to move aero engines and other equipment around the camp. The standard gauge system was steam powered until 1940 when the locos were replaced by 2 diesel shunting engines aptly named 'Ebb' and 'Flo'. The system was gradually run down and closed in December 1964. The station name was changed to Henlow Camp on 31 March 1933 reflecting the use the RAF made of the station. In December 1939 the platform was lengthened with a wooden extension to provide for wartime troop trains. These extra long trains were of eight coaches and were in use up until the 1960s. Hundreds of RAF personnel used the trains to head for London on a 36-hour leave pass. These trains left for King's Cross on Friday evenings and Saturday mornings and returned on Sunday nights.

Whilst carrying out research for this chapter the author received a letter from Mr and Mrs Hopkins of Rickmansworth.

The letter is self-explanatory.

Dear Mr Howard

I was on an engineering course at RAF technical college, Henlow from 1954 to 1957. My wife and I lived in married quarters, which was virtually next to the line where it ran through the camp. My wife had a part time job in Hitchin. She travelled to Hitchin and back on the train and became very friendly with the train crew. When she was pregnant – and not quite so quick on her feet – it was not unknown for the train crew to wait a little while whilst she came along the platform. After our son was born (now a father of two sons himself), my wife held him up for the train crew to see as they puffed past the married quarters. We almost always got a toot on the whistle when the train went by, even at night when it was dark and the curtains were drawn. How life has changed! Just a little thing, I know, but my wife and I remember those little things 45 years on and I wonder if the train crew are still with us? We are now in our 70s.

Yours sincerely
Keith and Irene Hopkins.

This letter reflects delightfully the mood of a typical quiet country railway, and the community spirit that existed at the time.

PLOWMAN'S SIDING.

Just to the north of Henlow there was another small railway system. This was Plowman's Siding, and opened in December 1893. Clay was extracted from a clay pit and transported on a narrow gauge tramway to a small brickworks. Train-loads of rubbish from London arrived on the main railway and were dumped in the pit.

The empty wagons were then filled with bricks from the brick works for the return journey to London. The author recalls fishing in this same pit in the early

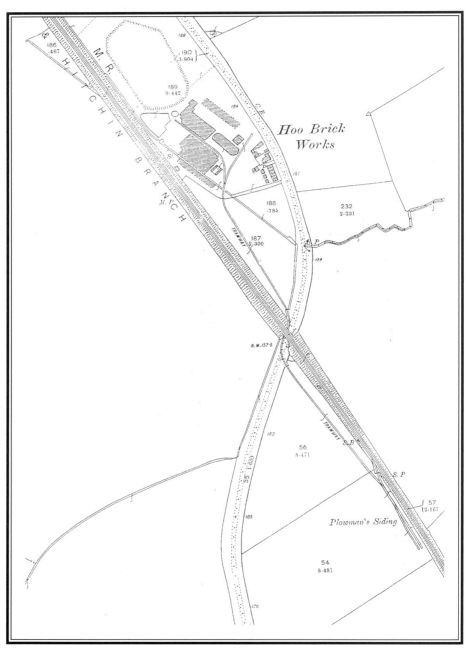

OS Map of 1900, showing the area around Plowman's Siding.

1990s named the Airman Pit. This was the same name as the public house just up the road on the junction with the Bedford road.

He remembers finding pieces of china in the fishing swims of the pit. These had coloured patterns on them and were probably brought here by the rubbish trains. Who knows, they were probably some part of a London Victorian family's dinner service!

SHEFFORD

Shefford station was next along the line and was unique in that it was of timber construction. Positioned at track level at the top of an embankment, it stood next to the bridge that carried the line over the main road. This meant that large timber beams had to be set into the embankment to support the station's structure.

The station was rebuilt in the 1940s, the replacement being a prefabricated concrete building at road level. Shefford had a small goods yard that handled a large amount of goods for its size and, along with other stations along the line, it had livestock pens and a coal yard. The coal yard was popular with the local population, as cheap coal was a direct result of the coming of the railways. Shefford station was demolished when the line closed. The importance of the railway serving Shefford is depicted in the town sign that incorporates a train.

Above: A special engineer's train crosses the bridge over Ampthill Road, Shefford, in the severe winter of 1962/3, to ensure the line was clear of snow. (Ivor Walton collection).
Below: The Shefford town sign depicting the Midland Railway in the bottom left corner. (Author)

There are some reminders of the railway as a pub named The Bridge stands next to the site of the bridge where the line once crossed the Ampthill road. Old Bridge Way and Old Station Way are two road names nearby. Also a cluster of houses built near to the old station in 1998 is named Midland Close.

With the exception of the Shefford to Southill section, the line was reduced to single track in 1911, due to lack of traffic and in order to reduce maintenance costs.

SOUTHILL

Southill station, in the late 1950s, looking towards Bedford, as a train approaches in the distance. (David Lawrence collection)

Southill was next along the line. The Whitbread family, famous for their brewing company, lived at Southill Park not far from the station. They had a private waiting room on the platform. William Whitbread's support for the line after campaigning for its opening was shown by his generosity.

He allowed a picnic to be held in his park for the passengers of one of the first trains to run on the opening day. His support for the line was acknowledged as in Southill Park a few hundred yards from the station a stone obelisk was erected in his honour. The inscription reads:

> "To William Henry Whitbread for his zeal and energy in promoting railways through the county of Bedford, 1864. Erected by public subscription".

Southill station building still exists today, having been converted into a private residence.

CARDINGTON

Cardington station was the last station along the line before reaching Bedford. The main passenger traffic for the station consisted of RAF personnel from nearby RAF Cardington. The camp is famous for its two enormous airship hangers,

The obelisk in Southill Park erected to the memory of William Henry Whitbread in recognition of his efforts in promoting railways through Bedfordshire. (Author)

from which the ill-fated airship R101 flew in 1930 before crashing in northern France with considerable loss of life.

Many troop trains left from Cardington during World War 2. The camp was used as a troop enrolment centre and troops were dispatched to various parts of the country for training.

The station is still in use today as business premises. The line then continued on into Bedford station where a bay platform was in use for Hitchin to Bedford branch trains.

PARTING OF THE WAYS.

The relationship between the Great Northern and the Midland was not a happy one. The GN gave priority to its own passenger and goods trains in preference to the Midland's.

Timetables became unreliable and many Bedford line passengers arriving at Hitchin missed their connections to London. Midland goods trains and coal trains sometimes arrived in London as much as two days late. Already, in 1861, a proposal had been made for a new line from London to Hitchin (see chapter 6) by-passing the GN.

The situation came to a head in June 1862 when there were 3,400 delays in that month alone. Pleading lack of space, the GN evicted the Midland from its sidings at King's Cross, and this became the last straw for the Midland.

The following year it applied for, and was granted, parliamentary powers to build a line from Bedford to London via Luton and St. Albans.

This line reached Moorgate Street in July 1868, and St. Pancras was opened in October of the same year.

By 1880 the Midland's new main line became so busy that it quadrupled the track to St. Pancras. A far cry from the congestion it had suffered at Hitchin. As a result, overnight, the Hitchin to Bedford Line lost its strategic importance.

Some odd forms of traction were used on the line in the few years before it closed. British Railways purchased three Park Royal railbuses. These were not a success on the line as they were mechanically unreliable. They were replaced by two-car diesel multiple units. These units were transferred for use elsewhere and steam came back into use on the line again.

Tank engines operated a "push and pull" service until the line finally closed. This service was affectionately called "The Billy Bedford" by locals and passengers alike ("push-and-pull" trains were sometimes used on branch lines to eliminate the need for the engine to run round the coaches at each change of direction. The engine remained coupled to one end of the train while, at the other, a driving cab contained controls mechanically linked to those on the engine). The last scheduled passenger train to Bedford steamed out of Hitchin on Saturday 30 December 1961. It was waved away from the platform by a small group of very cold enthusiasts.

The line had an unusual new lease of life in May 1964. The section between Bedford and Shefford was used to film some scenes for "Those Magnificent Men In Their Flying Machines".

An ex-Highland Railway locomotive, No 103, and a set of coaches were disguised as a train of the Nord Railway of France. In the film the actor Terry-Thomas accidentally lands his aircraft on the roof of the train. Before he can draw the driver's attention to stop

A two-coach 'push-and-pull' Bedford train waits to leave Hitchin 'down' platform in 1955, hauled by Ivatt 2-6-2T No 41270.
(Initial Photographics / B.W.L. Brooksbank)

*The Nightingale public house, formerly the Leicester Railway Inn,
photographed in 1999. In the foreground are the remains of the
Midland engine shed, prior to the construction of McDonalds. (Author)*

the train, his aircraft is smashed to pieces as the train goes into Warden tunnel.
A truly memorable scene.

The line closed completely on Christmas Eve 1964. The last train shunted at
Shefford station and left for Bedford.

Today little remains to remind us of this epic struggle to hasten to London.
The Midland goods shed still stands in Nightingale Road in a derelict and sorry
state. The engine shed survived for a number of years after the line closed,
being put to various uses. In 1974 the Department of the Environment carried
out a survey of the older buildings in Hitchin but, alas, looked upon the Midland
engine shed as having no historical interest. It did not think it worthy of making
it a listed building.

It was finally demolished in 1989. The engine shed and the engine turntable
became the site of a McDonald's fast food restaurant, built in 1999.
Unfortunately the Midland was not as fast as it wanted to be.

*A second class 'open'
single from Bedford
to Hitchin. The fare,
3s7d, is about 18p.
(Terry Knight
collection)*

THREE

HITCHIN STATION

H itchin soon began to expand further, as the impact of being an important railway junction began to take effect. The railway began recruiting local people, and their number soon swelled. Not only were there jobs for more common posts such as guards, drivers, shunters and platform staff, but also for lamplighters, wheeltappers, and "knocker uppers" who went around the town at all hours of the day and night awakening railway men for their duties. Few people had alarm clocks at this time.

These railway servants had to be housed, and several roads were built in the vicinity of the station to accommodate them. The most notable dwellings were built in Radcliffe Road, Dacre Road and Trevor Road, all close to the station. In Station Approach itself, a row of cottages was built and, on the other side of the railway, to the rear of the station, four further cottages were constructed. These two sets of cottages are still in use today. Although a certain amount of modernisation has taken place, their character has been preserved.

In 1874 Frederic Seebohm, a banker and local Quaker, made available part of the garden of his house, "The Hermitage" in Bancroft, to make access easier, along Hermitage Road, from the town to the station.

He certainly appreciated the coming of the railway as he is recorded as being one of Hitchin's first commuters to London, where he practised law in the 1850s. Hermitage Road was opened in 1875.

RELIGIOUS NEEDS FULFILLED

Several churches were built in the area to serve the religious needs of the ever-increasing population of railwaymen. In Radcliffe Road, Holy Saviour Church was built.

The funds for the building of the church were provided by the Reverend George Gainsford who wished, "to spend his wealth in this way to the glory of God, and because the increased population that came with the railways needed another place in the town". His wife laid the foundation stone on Ascension Day,

24 May 1864, and it was consecrated to the Holy Saviour a year later, on Ascension Day 1865. The service of consecration was carried out by Bishop Wigram of Rochester, in whose diocese the church was at the time.

Another notable place of worship was built in 1867. This was the Walsworth Baptist Mission which was a tin chapel built on land owned by Richard Johnson, the Chief Engineer of the Great Northern Railway. At the time many members of the congregation were railway employees and their families. A larger church of brick was constructed in 1875, and in 1914 a church hall replaced the original tin chapel. The hall has a foundation stone commemorating Richard Johnson's interest in the church. Johnson died in 1924 and is buried in Hitchin cemetery where a monument was dedicated to him and still stands today.

In more modern times, a room in the church was dedicated to him and aptly named the Richard Johnson Room. This room was opened on Sunday 11 October 1992 by the Reverend Malcolm Goodspeed, B.D., who at the time was the Baptist Union Secretary for the Ministry.

THE STATION TAKES SHAPE.

Further development took place around the station as the population of Hitchin increased from around 7,000 to 10,000 between 1850 and 1900. The area saw some of the highest land prices in the town up to the turn of the century.

The railway station itself soon became a shabby affair and after pressure from local passengers and Hitchin Urban District Council the Great Northern Railway put out contracts for extension and refurbishment. Works to extend

Just before the First World War, the western side of Hitchin station was remodelled to cater for increased traffic. The porte cochere survived until 1974 when it was demolished due to dry rot. (Hitchin Museum)

Railway workers pose in the forecourt of Hitchin Station, circa 1903. Behind them, in its original position, stands the Cabbies' Hut. (The Fells Family)

most of the buildings were started in June 1910 and completed by July 1911. One of the local station landmarks to be replaced was the footbridge. It was becoming unsafe, so a temporary bridge, opened on 10 October 1910, was built alongside the old one. The old bridge was then dismantled on 23 October 1910. Work began on a subway to link the platforms and thus replace the temporary bridge. The subway opened on 25 February 1911. In the same year, a station master's house was built in Station Approach, adjacent to the row of cottages, replacing the original one on the down platform.

At the end of 1910 work began on the construction of a new station entrance which was to be covered by a large canopy.

A new, larger booking hall was built to accommodate the ever increasing number of passengers using the station. During the construction of the canopy an accident occurred on New Year's Day 1914. A girder fell and brought down several others. A workman was severely injured, and taken to Hitchin Hospital, having been struck by one of the falling girders.

Adjacent to the entrance was a cabmen's shelter, which was erected in 1903. One of the most notable taxi proprietors of the day was Mr J Webb who was also licensee of the Coopers Arms public house. He is said to have had a thriving business, as in those days most people on market day had to come by train and he had the lion's share of the station yard business.

The building of the shelter was financed from donations, given by local rail users, collected by Edward Boxall who ran a cab business from The Red Lion in Bucklersbury. The Boxall family business continued down the generations, and the name can still be seen on taxis waiting outside Hitchin station to this day.

Mr Webb was not alone in the business of hired cabs. The Sun, The Swan and The Cock also hired cabs and "flies", a one-horse Hackney Carriage. A contractor in Bancroft set up as a "shillibeer" proprietor (a shillibeer was a single-deck horse bus, named after its inventor).

The shelter was a familiar sight until 1976, when it was removed to a local private garden. In 1998 it was restored and relocated in the Market Square, the restoration project (see Chapter 7) being organised by the Hitchin Historical Society.

The entrance to the station had restricted access due to a grass triangle of land owned by the Great Northern Railway. The Hitchin Urban District Council approached the company with a view to reaching an agreement to improve access. Much to the surprise of the council the GNR surrendered the land to the council subject to certain conditions. These were that no buildings be erected, the surface metalled, and a centre light be erected to throw light onto the roadway – an unusual extravagance in those days. These works were completed in September 1913.

THE TOWN AND INDUSTRY BENEFITS

As the town began to grow, goods traffic on the railway increased. One of the first industries to take advantage of the railway was the gas works. This was originally built in 1834 at the junction of Nightingale Road and Grove Road. It moved next to the railway in 1904 so that coal could be delivered directly by rail. The Hertfordshire iron works was also built adjacent to the gas works. Some of

A general view of Hitchin station looking north from Benslow Bridge in 1911.
(From an original postcard)

One of Ransom's twenty private owner open wagons for transporting lime.
The spelling of Ransom's name with a final 'e' is a mystery as yet unsolved.
(Historical Model Railway Photograph Collection)

the gas works buildings in Cooks Way were in use until recently, converted to various industrial uses. Several sidings were provided for various industries that were prominent at the time. One of these sidings went into a lime works under the chalk cliff below Benslow Hill. This works was owned and run by Alfred Ransom (later by his son Theodore) and the lime produced by the kilns was used mainly by the building industry.

There was also Greystone Lime Works to the north of the station, at the end of Cadwell Lane as it is known today. Local legend has it that several tramps met an untimely death at these lime works in Cadwell Lane. In the winter months, to escape from the cold, they sneaked into the works and made a bed up next to the warm kilns. They died during the night as a result of the noxious fumes produced during the lime making process. This lime works was adjacent to Barker's timber yard and saw mill. It was a not uncommon sight to see the sidings almost full of wagons of timber waiting either to be processed in the mill or for distribution on the railway system to various parts of the country.

The countryside around Hitchin was a prime area for farming, the main produce being wheat crops. Much of this wheat was traded by T.W.P. Franklin, a coal, corn and seed merchant. A large warehouse building owned by this firm contained milling machinery, which stood for a long time in a dilapidated state, in Nightingale Road opposite B&Q. To serve the needs of such grain merchants the Corn Exchange, built in 1853, became a hive of activity with grain merchants

*The disused Franklin's flour mill in Nightingale Road, prior to demolition in 2003.
(Author)*

coming from various parts of the country to trade with dealers. Much of the grain was moved by rail to various locations around the country. Some trains consisted solely of grain wagons.

To accommodate this traffic, and much other freight, goods shunting yards were provided on both sides of the line, just north of the station. The yard on the up (London) side was the busiest, with shunting of wagons going on all day.

Goods traffic was not the only commodity to increase at the time.

The GNR laid on many Sunday excursions to the seaside, which were well patronised by local townspeople.

There were also some midweek excursions. For example, a day excursion to Skegness on Thursday 16 September 1914 departed Hitchin at 6.20am and returned at 7.50pm. A long day!

There were, however, people who disapproved of Sunday excursions such as a writer to the Hitchin Baptist and Congregational Magazine in the summer of 1921 who complained:

> "What a pity it is that the GNR have started Sunday excursions. Surely there is no excuse for this in these days! Everybody seems to have all the necessary leisure during the six days of the week, and why should the servants of the Railway Company have to give up their Sunday rest to take people to the coast that could very well go on a weekday? It seems a great piece of folly. We hope wiser counsel will soon prevail and this sort of thing will be nipped in the bud."

The author of the letter could not have known how much railwaymen at the time appreciated these excursions, as it bought them much needed overtime to raise their pay to a living wage.

PASSENGER NEEDS

Passengers arriving at Hitchin had quite a selection of accommodation close to the station if they wished to find a room for the night. Adjacent to the station entrance was "The Railway Inn", later called "The Station Hotel". This had a stable block at the rear reached through a carriage arch. The hotel was again renamed in the 1960s "The Talisman", the name of an important express train that passed through Hitchin at that time. It was renamed again to "Jeans", before being damaged by fire and demolished in the late 1980s.

An office block, "Lyon Court", now stands on the site of "The Talisman". Further round the comer from the station in Nightingale Road was "The Railway Junction".

This hostelry was a well-known 'watering hole' for local railwaymen who, after a session with their mates, could honestly tell their wives that they were late home, having been "held up at the Junction". The inn was sold in June 1962 to James Bowman and Sons who had a flour mill next door. The inn was converted to a mess room and canteen for Bowman's employees.

A B&Q DIY store was built in 1985 on the site of Bowman's Mill. A few yards further along Nightingale Road stood "The Leicester Railway Inn", which derived its name from the Midland branch line to Bedford and beyond to Leicester.

It was renamed "The Nightingale", as it is known today. The modem fascia boards cover the original name, set in concrete, as noticed recently when the front of "The Nightingale" was revamped.

"TEMPORARY PLATFORM" ON THE UP SIDE.

In 1974 the platform on the up side needed to be lengthened to accommodate longer trains with the electrification of the line. As this work necessitated the dismantling of part of the "up" platform, a temporary platform was required for the duration of the work.

This temporary platform was constructed of scaffold and wooden planks at the rear of the "up" platform. Access to the temporary platform was through a door at the rear of the "up" platform adjacent to the top of the subway steps.

The platform was in use for a month in November until the works were complete. To serve the platform, trains were diverted off the "up" slow line round the back of the "up" platform to the temporary platform.

They then continued on and rejoined the slow line just before Benslow Bridge. After serving its purpose, the platform was left in situ for some time before it was dismantled.

SUPPORT DEPARTMENTS

Support department buildings behind Hitchin's 'up' side platform, photographed in 1973. (Roy Revell collection)

No railway would be able to function without the necessary support departments. Amongst these were the signal fitters and signal & telegraph departments. These departments were responsible for the servicing and repair of signals and electrical circuits and also the internal telephone system. The departments were situated at the rear of the up platform with road access from Cambridge Road up the slope by St Michael's Mount cottages. At this site there were also buildings for gas fitters, carpenters, plumbers and a mess room.

HITCHIN'S CONTRIBUTION TO A SAFER RAILWAY

A serious accident occurred on the GNR at Abbots Ripton, between Huntingdon and Peterborough, on 21 January 1876 in which 13 people were killed and 24 injured. The accident occurred when one train ran into another after passing a signal in the all clear position, when in fact it should have been at danger. The winter conditions at the time froze the signal arm into its slot in the signal post causing it to jam in the clear position. As a result of this accident, a Hitchin signal inspector, Edward French, designed a centre-balance signal arm to overcome the problems encountered with the slotted signals which were in common use at the time. In September 1877 he took out a provisional patent for his signal. In those days, the idea of an individual employed by the railway taking out a patent for an idea was frowned upon by his managers. Instead of getting any credit for his invention, he instead received a sharp "rap over the knuckles". The situation was made even more unpleasant for him when a potential financial backer withdrew his support, rather than be further involved. It must have been intensely frustrating for French to see signals of the kind he had invented being used, before long, as standard throughout the GNR. This is the unhappy origin of the "somersault arm signal" that became a feature of the line for almost a hundred years.

HITCHIN'S SIGNAL BOXES
Hitchin's importance as a busy main line and station meant that four signal boxes were required to supervise the passage of trains.

HITCHIN SOUTH
The first box was called Hitchin South, and was situated just south of Benslow Bridge. The box opened in June 1894 and had a 55-lever frame. This box not only dealt with the passing of trains on the main line but also movements in and out of the engineers' yard, the locomotive shed and the cattle dock sidings. The box closed on 16 December 1975. A very serious accident occurred near the south box in 1959 involving several goods trains, which blocked the line for over a day. A detailed account of this accident appears in chapter 5.

Hitchin South box seen through Benslow Bridge in 1974. Note the earthworks on the left just prior to the bridge being demolished on 28 July that year. (Roy Revell collection)

HITCHIN YARD

The second and busiest signal box was the Hitchin Yard box which was opened in February 1878 and had a 45 lever frame, the box being built at the end of the down platform. Not only was it responsible for the passing of main line trains but movements in and out of both goods yards.

Up until December 1961 trains from Bedford arrived at Hitchin at the up platform. Before they could return to Bedford they had to cross over all four lines to get to the down side, before reversing into the down platform ready for departure. This was quite a complicated move conducted between the passage of normal trains and, needless to say, trains sometimes left Hitchin for Bedford behind time.

The box was at its busiest during the day and thus two signalmen were on duty much of the time with a telegraph lad employed to fill in the train log as the signalmen were busy signalling the passing of trains. Behind the Yard box was a short siding called the fish dock where fish wagons were unloaded. It also served as a waiting siding for the train to Bedford, which normally consisted of a tank engine and one coach in steam days. Just before it was due to leave, the train went out onto the down slow line and reversed onto the down platform ready for departure to Bedford. The Yard box closed on the 16 November 1974.

Hitchin Yard box, looking north, in the 1960s. (George Howe collection)

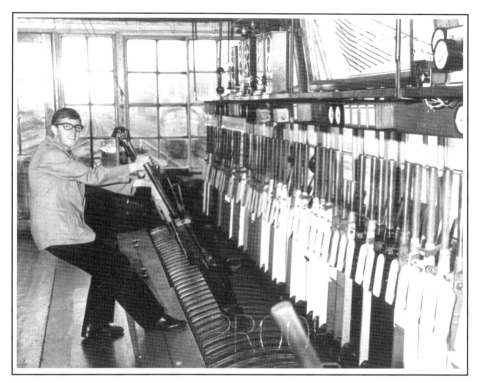

Hitchin Signalman Vaughan Bloom at work in Cambridge Junction box during the 1960s. A train in the background is taking the branch to Cambridge. (Comet Group Newspapers)

HITCHIN CAMBRIDGE JUNCTION

A third box was located just north of the station where a branch line to Cambridge left the main line. This box was called the Cambridge Junction box. It opened in June 1878 and had a 62-lever frame. This signal box supervised movements onto the Cambridge branch and also signalled the passing of main line trains and movements in and out of the diesel depot. It closed on 16 January 1977.

HITCHIN MIDLAND

A fourth box was opposite the Cambridge junction box. This was Hitchin Midland box and dealt exclusively with Midland trains moving on and off the Bedford branch. It was a common sight to see the Midland's station master walking along the track from his office in his full uniform on his way to visit the box. Twice a day he made the trip to sign the train log and to see all was well with the signalman and the Midland infrastructure. The box closed on 9 August 1964.

CADWELL BOX

Another signal box worthy of note was situated one and a half miles north of Hitchin at Cadwell Crossing. This crossing was where the Icknield Way crossed the main line. The box opened in December 1870 and had a 25-lever frame.

One of the signalmen who manned the box lived in a small bungalow opposite the box adjacent to the main line. The signalbox and bungalow, being in such an isolated location, had no mains services. Water churns and lamp oil were dropped off each day by a passing goods train that shunted the goods yards along the route between Hitchin and Huntingdon. If the regular signalman was off duty his relief signalman had a long walk to the box, the nearest road being the road through the village of Ickleford, a distance of half a mile away!

The box closed on 29 June 1969.

None of the signalboxes in the Hitchin area remains; all signalling is now controlled from a modern signalling centre at King's Cross.

The Author recalls many trainspotting trips to the crossing from his home in Letchworth with some of his school-mates, in the sixties. The most interesting time was in the summer months when the signalbox windows were open. Approaching trains were signalled by bell codes so it was possible to tell which sort of train was approaching before it reached the crossing. The worst part was the cycle ride home to Letchworth, cycling uphill along the Icknield Way up to the Wilbury Hotel then onto the Grange Estate.

With the advent of high-speed trains it became obvious that it was too dangerous to have the public crossing the lines on foot. To this end a footbridge was built across the line replacing the crossing. The footbridge was constructed and came into use in 2000; thus again another local landmark disappeared into history.

PERMANENT WAY MAINTENANCE.

The railway itself had to be maintained and, to facilitate this, an engineers' yard was built to the south of Benslow Bridge to the south of the station.

The Hitchin firm of G.H. Innes and Company, iron founders, won the contract to build the yard and workshops on 6 January 1914 and work began on 14 January 1914.

This yard was affectionately called "The Farm" by railwaymen, probably as a farm was previously on the site, and the name stuck until its closure.

The first engine entered the newly constructed yard on 5 June 1916.

As the yard became busier the entrance points were connected to the South signalbox on 20 June 1917. The yard had many sidings that contained wagons with material for track replacement and point repair.

The yard became particularly busy on Thursdays and Fridays as engineers' wagons were shunted into trains for specific tasks that were undertaken on Sundays when the passage of trains was quieter.

For example, if a length of track needed replacing on the main line anywhere

Class A4 Pacific 'Mallard' passes Cadwell signal box on a London-bound express, during the 1950's.
(Initial Photographics / H.D. Ramsey)

Class A4 Pacific 60029 'Woodcock' passes Hitchin South box, passing from the down fast to the down slow, in April 1959. Note 'The Farm' engineers' yard in the background. (Michael Joyce collection)

between Langley Junction, just south of Stevenage, and Wood Green, trains on the main line could be diverted around the work site. They left the main line at Langley, travelled via Hertford North and continued on to rejoin the main line at Wood Green. Trains departing King's Cross also took this same route travelling via Hertford North.

Several "lengthmen" were employed throughout the area, to walk along a specific length of track to check for broken rails and any other defects that may have occurred with the track and sleepers. They were a familiar sight walking along the track with a large spanner over their shoulder tightening any fish plate bolts that may have come loose.

If a broken rail was found this was reported immediately and the section of track closed until it was repaired. This caused obvious delays to trains, as they could not use the affected line. A mad dash then occurred at the engineers' yard to load a wagon with a replacement rail. A locomotive was sent to the yard from the locomotive shed to proceed with the rail to the site of the broken rail, which was quickly replaced to allow the line to reopen.

With the advent of long welded rail a section of track could be laid sometimes a mile long. This rail was virtually maintenance free and the engineers' yard gradually declined due to lack of work and closed in 1995.

The land that it occupied was sold for housing development and Fairview New Homes Ltd built houses on the site, completed in 1998.

The development was called the Hillview Estate but still keeps its railway connection as the roads have various railway names, such as Talisman Street, Wedgewood (sic) Way and Pullman Drive to name but a few.

(See Appendix 1 for a full list of the street names, and an explanation of their railway connections.)

Beyond this estate is the Poets' Estate, the land for which also belonged at one time to the GNR. Their intention was to build more marshalling yards and a steam locomotive works on the site but this never came about. Who knows? If this had been the case Hitchin may have become another railway centre, competing with Doncaster or Darlington!

Hitchin station platform ticket – note the incorrectly reversed BR logo! (Terry Knight collection)

FOUR

HITCHIN LOCO SHED

itchin, being roughly half way between London and Peterborough, became a natural place for an engine service facility. The locomotives of the 1850s were limited in the distance they could travel before refuelling, so Hitchin was an ideal location for coal and water supplies.

An engine shed was constructed and came into use on 7 August 1850, the same day as the opening of the King's Cross to Peterborough main line. The shed had two tracks, and was built to the south of the station, behind the up platform. It was a brick-built shed measuring 120ft x 25ft with a single gable slated roof. A coke fuelling stage was erected and positioned so that it could fuel an engine either in the shed yard or standing at the head of a train in the up platform.

On 1 July 1851, a 40ft engine turntable was authorised, being sited to the east of the shed. The GNR Locomotive Engineer at the time was Archibald Sturrock and, as such, he was responsible for Hitchin Loco Shed. As the shed became more and more busy, additional items were required. Sturrock applied to the GNR's Executive Committee for an additional water crane on the up platform. This was agreed for the sum of £85. It also became apparent that if a derailment occurred there were no facilities for re-railing. To this end an 8 ton hand-operated crane was provided and formed part of a breakdown train. On 3 March 1861, Sturrock applied again to the committee for a new ash pit, two sidings and an additional water crane, all of which were approved. He also had the engine shed lengthened to 160ft in March 1865.

WATER SUPPLY

The water supply for the water cranes situated around the site was obtained from a pump house adjacent to the shed, which pumped water from two wells sunk into the ground.

The two pumps were steam driven and the tall chimney towering above the pump house was a familiar landmark at this end of the town.

The pumps supplied water for a 12,000 gallon tank, which was gravity fed to the site. The annual consumption at this time was 8,000,000 gallons. As the existing pumps were struggling to keep up with demand, Sturrock applied again

Above: Hitchin engine shed in 1866. Note the chimney above the pump house, and the turntable pit on the right. (Hitchin Museum)
Below: A general view of Hitchin shed in 1958. Note the water crane at the end of the platform, and the water softening plant tank in the background. (Michael Joyce collection)

for additional funding, this time for £670, which provided for an additional pump house, pumping engine, pumps, and a water crane.

SHED IDENTIFICATION

Several times in the following chapters, mention is made of locomotives allocated to Hitchin. To indicate to which shed an engine belonged, a shed identification was displayed on each engine. The term "shed" had by now come to mean the entire locomotive servicing facility, as well as the individual building in which engines were housed.

In GNR times (until 1923) locomotives displayed a small metal disc, usually on the cab top sheeting. This disc did not show the actual shed, but instead identified the main shed "district" to which a number of sub-sheds belonged. Hitchin was a sub shed in district No. 3, the main shed being London, King's Cross.

The GNR became part of the London and North Eastern Railway (LNER) in 1923, and from November 1924 engines in the Southern area, which included Hitchin, began to have white enamelled plates with the shed name in black on the inside of the cab roof, usually on the right hand side. These plates were not easily seen from ground level, so a new means of shed identification was brought into use in December 1938. This time the name of the shed was painted on the front buffer beam of each locomotive.

With nationalisation of the Railways in 1948, British Railways introduced a new system of identification where each motive power district was given a number followed by a letter for each shed, or group of sheds. Hitchin came under the London (King's Cross) District, and was coded 34D. The identifying shed code was displayed on a small elliptical cast metal plate on the front of the smoke box door of each locomotive.

LOCOMOTIVE NUMBERS INCREASE

As the frequency of trains increased, so did the number of locomotives allocated to Hitchin shed. It is recorded that John Budge, the King's Cross superintendent, visited Hitchin in August 1866 to check on the locomotives because of complaints about time keeping. He found eleven locomotives working and only one stopped for repairs, number 21, a Sharps tank engine. This was under repair with a leaking firebox. The locomotives were averaging 105 miles a day each, an extensive distance by the standards of the day. Budge complained about the variety of locomotives at the shed. Some of these locomotives were more powerful than others, all likely to run the same trains, hence the variable punctuality.

It was not until 1869 that further locomotives were built at Doncaster. Nine years after Budge's visit, Stirling's famous 8ft singles arrived in the London area and by November 1875 one of them was a regular visitor to Hitchin. It worked mainly on slow stopping trains from King's Cross to Hitchin and, between trains, was stabled on Hitchin shed.

As the years passed, larger locomotives were allocated to Hitchin's shed. One of these types was the Ivatt "Atlantic" with 4-4-2 wheel arrangement. The turntable was increased in size, this time to 60ft in diameter. This larger turntable was commissioned in 1905 and was built by Ransome and Rapier. It was repositioned further east of the shed, which meant an opening had to be excavated in the chalk to make room for the turntable pit.

The repositioning of the turntable had an extra bonus as it opened up the entrance to the shed, which until then had been somewhat restricted.

STEAM RAILCARS

A different type of traction arrived at Hitchin in April 1907: steam railcars, consisting of a single carriage body with a small conventional-looking steam loco permanently attached at one end.

These "Railmotors" were built at GNR's own Doncaster works and elsewhere, six in all, three of which are known to have worked from Hitchin. Another type of steam railcar was also at Hitchin.

These railcars were manufactured by Clayton Wagons Limited of Lincoln. They were unsightly-looking devices, with the engine being inside the coach body, with a small coal-bunker outside the body at the engine end. Their seating capacity was 64 passengers and they were used on the Hitchin to Baldock shuttle service. Steam railcars were also used on the Hertford to Stevenage line when the loop from Wood Green to Hertford North was extended to Stevenage in June 1924.

There were five trains a day from Hertford North to Stevenage calling at the intermediate stations of Stapleford and Watton-at-Stone.

A TRADE UNION IS FORMED

Another notable date in 1907 was Sunday 15 September, when a union branch was formed at Hitchin. Two officials of the King's Cross branch of "The Associated Society of Locomotives Engineers and Firemen" (ASLEF) contacted Hitchin, and a meeting was arranged at St Saviour's Club premises which were lent for the purpose by the Rev. George Bernard Gainsford who, it is quoted, was "a gentleman who takes a great interest in everything connected with the locomotives, including the men who manipulate them, and that is unusual in these days". A Mr Dickinson of the King's Cross Branch presided at the meeting and, after he had explained the advantages of the Society, Mr A. Smith was appointed Hitchin Branch Secretary. Such was the interest in the Society that the first branch meeting was held a week later on 22 September.

"MODERNISATION" TAKES PLACE

Gradually the conditions for railwaymen improved, but one particular problem at Hitchin needed to be addressed: that of the ashpits. H. N. Gresley, then the GNR's Locomotive Engineer, commented in March 1919: "The enginemen at

Riddles J94 0-6-0 saddle-tank No 68073 at the mechanical coaling plant during the 1950s. The coal tubs in the foreground are ready to be lifted to tip the coal into a locomotive tender. (Basil Coles collection)

Hitchin have complained from time to time about the lack of simple pit accommodation for the preparation, examination and inspection of locomotives. At the moment there are 29 engines stationed at Hitchin and only covered pit accommodation for 5. Now that the engine-men's hours have been reduced from 10 to 8, it is necessary to turn more engines round at Hitchin than was formerly the case, with the result that the shortage of pit accommodation will become more acute." As a result of this, Gresley proposed the existing pit be extended by 49 ft and an additional pit be built outside the shed. The expenditure for this project was approved in April 1919.

In the early 1920s the number of locomotives allocated to Hitchin was 34, operated by 66 crews of engine men. Some additional improvements were proposed at the time because of the conditions "not conducive to economical and efficient working." Among these improvements were separate inlet and outlet tracks from the shed, a mechanical coaling plant and twelve 10cwt tubs, with coal shelter and coalmen's cabin. The quantity of coal being consumed at the time was 20,000 tons per annum, so a new coaling plant would certainly improve the coaling facilities and save time and backache! The new coaling plant scheme was approved in January 1928. The LNER accepted a tender for the plant from the firm of Stothert and Pitt of Bath. The coaling plant was of girder construction and was installed at the south end of the locomotive yard, and the suggested improvements to shed lines were also carried out.

The allocation of locomotives fluctuated for a while. In 1931 the strength was 25, which included two railmotors used for the Hertford North shuttle and the Cambridge branch. These units were named "Rising Sun" and "Expedition".

WATER SUPPLIES REVISITED

Also during the 1930s, the locomotive shed was re-roofed and a water softening plant built. The softening plant provided water to the various water cranes around the site including the platforms. Bags of lime and soda ash were mixed with water in the plant. Softened water did not scale up the boiler tubes of locomotives which had been a problem with hard water in the past.

50TH ANNIVERSARY OF THE "FLYING SCOTSMAN"

A momentous occasion took place in Hitchin on 30 June 1938. The London and North Eastern Railway Information Agent at the time, Mr E. G. Marsden, thought of a way to commemorate the 50th anniversary of the "Flying Scotsman" train service.

His idea was to run the preserved Stirling 8ft single "No 1" alongside a modern day locomotive of the time, A4 Pacific number 4498, "Sir Nigel Gresley". No 1 was taken from York Museum to Doncaster works for an overhaul to prepare it for mainline running on 13 June 1938. It transpired that little work was required to bring the locomotive into running order. A train was formed for the

Stirling 8ft Single locomotive 'No 1' at Hitchin, after the anniversary run in 1938.
(Comet Newspaper Group)

A4 Pacific locomotive 'Sir Nigel Gresley' passes Hitchin, en route to Grantham with the 'Flying Scotsman' train in June 1938. (Comet Newspaper Group)

old locomotive consisting of seven vintage Great Northern six-wheel coaches, suitably decorated. The two trains formed up adjacent to each other at King's Cross. At 2pm on 30 June, No 1 steamed out of King's Cross and stopped at Stevenage, where its passengers transferred to the new "Flying Scotsman" pulled by "Sir Nigel Gresley", which was standing alongside. There were many enthusiasts and press photographers at Stevenage to witness the occasion. Sir Nigel Gresley himself hurried down onto the track side to take photographs of the two locomotives standing side by side. No 4498 then left Stevenage with the new "Flying Scotsman" for Barkston – near Grantham – where the train reversed on the triangular junction before its return journey to London.

"No 1" then ran on with its vintage train to Hitchin, where the locomotive was turned before returning to London, watched from the chalk cliff behind the loco shed by a large crowd.

THE SECOND WORLD WAR AND BEYOND

The Second World War was a busy time for Hitchin locomotives. Over and above their normal passenger and freight workings they assisted with numerous troop trains, many of which went on to RAF Henlow, on the Bedford branch. A strange

Above: An unidentified Gresley Pacific passing trainspotters perched on the remains of the down-side air-raid shelter, opposite the loco shed, during the 1950s (Anonymous donor)
Left: The up side air raid shelter, circa 2000. (Scilla Douglas)

visitor to Hitchin shed was a class F4 tank engine, number 7172. This locomotive was armour clad, designed for work with coastal defence units. It arrived at Hitchin in June 1940 and stayed until May 1943 but the armour cladding was never to be put to the test, and the loco returned to normal service.

For the protection of railway staff, two large air raid shelters were built near the station. The first was constructed near the chalk cliff adjacent to the loco shed, on the up side of the line; the second behind the down platform. This latter shelter became a good vantage point for trainspotters over the years. The author recalls sitting on the roof of the shelter during the 1960s watching the trains go by. Access to the roof was by clambering up the chalk bank behind the shelter, then jumping across onto the roof. Being opposite the loco shed, this favoured location gave excellent views of both locos on shed and passing trains.

Just after the war, Hitchin saw the arrival of several classes of locomotive to replace its ageing stock. The most numerous of these was the Thompson B1 tender engine, a general purpose locomotive used mainly on suburban stopping trains. Whenever possible, one of these locomotives was kept to one side, ready in steam to assist any main line locomotives that failed on passing express trains. This standby locomotive was referred to as the station "pilot", a term used for a

Hitchin Fireman John Toddington at the controls of failed A4 Pacific 'Wild Swan' on Hitchin Shed in the early 1960s. (John Toddington collection)

loco on duty for general (mostly shunting stock) duties. The B1s became popular at Hitchin, with 14 out of 30 locomotives on the shed being B1s at nationalisation, which took place on 1 January 1948.

Driver John Toddington of Hitchin shed recalls, when he was a fireman, a notable failure of an express train at Hitchin in the early 1960s. A Gresley A4 Pacific locomotive 60021, "Wild Swan" failed on the down main line in Hitchin Station. The A4 was shunted into the loco shed and the shed pilot was coupled to the train to continue its journey north.

To have a main line loco on the shed was a rarity, and the staff of the shed took the opportunity to inspect the loco at close quarters. Fitters attended to the A4 and found the water injectors were not working properly. On closer inspection it was found that water was not getting through from the tender to the locomotive boiler due to a partial blockage. It was found that some paper had blocked the outlet port in the tender, restricting the water flow. The drain cocks on the tender were opened to drain the tender and a fitter had to climb down inside the tender to remove the offending paper. Once the tender was refilled it was ready for service again. Fireman Toddington fired the A4 on a stopping goods train to Peterborough (the saying "using a hammer to crack a walnut" springs to mind), so that the locomotive could get back to its normal diagrammed working of express passenger trains.

Another class of locomotive, designed by Thompson, was the L1 2-6-4 tank engine. By 1950, nine of this class were allocated to the Hitchin shed. They were affectionately known as "concrete mixers" because of the clanking noise they made, especially when they were coasting. The first sign that steam traction was soon to be on the decline came in December 1957, when the first diesel locomotive, a shunter, arrived at Hitchin.

Diesel power replaces steam

In April 1960 work started on a new diesel depot on the site of the old Midland goods yard in Nightingale Road. The depot provided facilities for servicing diesel locomotives, which included pits between the two tracks that ran into the depot.

In the same year as the diesel era dawned, the number of steam locomotives dwindled to 12 at Hitchin. These were gradually transferred to New England shed at Peterborough or to King's Cross. The steam shed finally closed in June 1961, two months short of its 111th anniversary. On the diesel front, the number of locomotives allocated to Hitchin increased to thirteen main line locomotives and six diesel shunters.

Although the steam shed had officially closed the facilities were still kept in working order. Until the summer of 1963, Hitchin was the southern limit of steam operation; steam locomotives were serviced there before returning north.

Probably the last steam locomotive to use the turntable at Hitchin was a Great Western engine, 7029 "Clun Castle". The locomotive was in the area on a rail tour special, and came to Hitchin to be turned. Several engine crews on duty at the time, including the author, assisted in pushing the locomotive round on the turntable. The engine shed was demolished but the turntable remained serviceable until the late 1970s, when it was taken out and removed to the Buckinghamshire Railway Centre at Quainton Road, north of Aylesbury, to begin a new lease of life.

Diesel traction arrives

The diesel allocation at Hitchin consisted of four types of locomotive. The first were affectionately known as Baby Deltics. These locomotives were built by the English Electric Company. They proved to be underpowered at 1,100 horsepower, only a third of the power of their big brother Deltics which were 3,300 horsepower, and worked the main line express trains on the East Coast route. The Baby Deltics were used mainly on "outer suburban" services such as King's Cross to Baldock or Royston stopping at intermediate stations. They worked the occasional freight train and were often coupled together to form a "double header" on Sunday engineers' trains.

A more successful and reliable general-purpose locomotive type, working alongside the Baby Deltics, was the Brush Type "2" locomotive. They were manufactured by the Brush Traction Company, Loughborough and most were

An English Electric Type 1 locomotive shunts wagons at Cadwell sidings near Ickleford in 1964. (John Toddington collection)

1,365 horsepower. This class of locomotive became so popular that over 260 were built and distributed over the national rail network and, although their numbers have dwindled, some are still in use today. Both the Baby Deltic and Brush Type '2' locomotives were fitted with oil fired boilers that were used to steam-heat passenger trains, the carriages of which were fitted with steam pipes throughout.

The main type of locomotive at Hitchin for freight and shunting duties was the English Electric Type 1. They proved to be very reliable workhorses on freight trains and were often used to shunt goods yards in the area: Biggleswade, Sandy, and St Neots being examples. They were most useful as a pair, coupled together nose to nose, so that the driver's view from the cab at the rear was not obstructed by their characteristic long bodies.

ELECTRIFICATION ARRIVES

By the early 1970s various main lines around the country were being converted to electric power provided by overhead power wires. The West Coast route electrification from Euston to Glasgow was completed in May 1974, so it was thought the East Coast route would follow before long. The suburban electrification from Moorgate and King's Cross to Welwyn Garden City, Hertford North and Royston came into operation in October 1977. This marked the beginning of the end of diesel traction at Hitchin, and the locomotives were gradually phased out and moved away.

As a result of the electrification preparations Benslow Bridge, a familiar Hitchin landmark, disappeared overnight on 28 July 1974. This single span brick-built bridge, constructed in 1850, spanned the line just south of Hitchin, adjacent to Hitchin South signal box. Its roadway was narrow, the bridge having been built to carry horse-drawn traffic.

It was, over the years, a familiar place for train spotters, and many photos of passing trains were taken from this vantage point. It finally succumbed to demolition at 1.37am on 1 August 1974, when it was blown up. The legacy of the bridge still lives on to this day as a modern equivalent footbridge was constructed a few yards south of the original site.

Many other familiar landmarks including the gas lamps that illuminated the engine shed and surrounding walkways were disconnected and dismantled in early 1978. Most of these had been in constant use since the shed was built in 1850!

Although the diesel depot in Nightingale Road became redundant, the building soon had a new lease of life. It became a stabling and service facility for rail maintenance units. Most of these are self-propelled and are used to level the track and to pack ballast around the sleepers. They are mainly used at night and weekends when the rail system is at its quietest.

Nothing remains of the steam shed today. On the site a Royal Mail Distribution Depot was built, and which is now in its turn disused.

A Brush Type 2 locomotive passes Hitchin South box with the 'Cambridge Buffet Express' during the 1960s. In the background, a train of new rail sections is ready for despatch from the engineers' yard. (George Howe collection)

The main purpose of this depot was to serve the two Travelling Post Office (TPO) trains that used to call at Hitchin in the early hours of the morning, one going North and the other South. The coaches of these trains were mobile sorting offices. The mail was sorted en route, and dropped off at various stations it was booked to call at along the line.

These TPOs were a familiar sight at Hitchin in the early hours of the morning. There was a flurry of activity as scores of mail bags were loaded and unloaded to speed the departure of the train. In 1996 Royal Mail, in order to save money, axed the northbound TPO that stopped at Hitchin, en route to Newcastle.

In 2003 Royal Mail decided to start to phase out all TPOs to save money, and the mail was transferred to road and aircraft for distribution around the country. In 2004 the southbound TPO to London suffered the same fate; the last mail train to leave Hitchin for London left at 1.30am on Saturday 10 January. The rest of the site remained overgrown and derelict until very recently – see chapter 8.

A B12 4-6-0 stands on the Great Northern turntable during the 1950s, while a J6 0-6-0 waits outside the steam shed at the rear. (Anonymous donor)

SIGNALS AT DANGER

Most railway junctions throughout the country have suffered some sort of accident during their history. Hitchin is no exception. An accident occurred on 3 August 1851, barely a year after the line had opened.

A down goods train was passing Stevenage when the driver, a man by the name of Bradley, realised his locomotive was short of water.

He whistled to the guard to apply the brakes on the guard's van, to assist in stopping the train. Bradley uncoupled his engine from the train and proceeded to Hitchin to take on water.

While he was filling the engine he saw in the distance, to his horror, his own train bearing down on him. The guard's brake had not been sufficient to hold the train on the gradient. Bradley decided to run his engine into a siding, thus allowing his train to pass, but time was against him. The runaway train collided with the locomotive, pushing it into the siding, through the buffer-stops and down an embankment. Driver Bradley was disciplined for his actions, being reduced to the rank of fireman.

AN EARLY ACCIDENT ON THE MIDLAND

Another accident happened at Hitchin just after 10pm on 8 September 1859 involving a train coming off the Midland line from Bedford, which had been opened just two years earlier.

This time the accident was attributed to a signalman's error. The late-running Midland train was coming off the branch towards Hitchin station under clear signals. A down Scotch express (railwaymen have always traditionally referred to main line trains between London and Scotland as "Scotch" expresses) was ready to leave Hitchin, and the signalman decided to give this train priority.

He set the signals against the Midland train but it was too late, as the train had already passed the signal. It collided head-on with the departing Scotch express, fortunately at a relatively slow speed. The Midland train was only slightly damaged but two coaches of the Scotch express were derailed resulting in 35 passengers being slightly injured.

COLLISION ON THE GREAT NORTHERN

In 1876, an accident occurred at Arlesey, just north of Hitchin. It was the afternoon before Christmas Eve. At this time trains were very crowded with people journeying away for the Christmas period. The 2.45pm Manchester express became so popular that it was decided to run the train in two portions from King's Cross. The first portion left King's Cross on time, with Driver Pepper in charge. He was unaware of the disaster that was to unfold in front of him and his train.

Further north along the main line a pick-up goods train had reached Arlesey with 26 wagons at 3.30pm. The Arlesey signalman placed his signals at danger to protect this move. The goods train started its shunt movement, crossing the main line, into Arlesey sidings. As it did so four of the wagons derailed on the crossover points, blocking the main line.

The express was travelling at 55mph approaching Arlesey when the driver saw the Arlesey signals at danger. He immediately applied his brakes and whistled for the guard to do the same at the rear of the train. With his train fully loaded, Driver Pepper had no chance of stopping in such a short distance. Realising a collision was imminent, Driver Pepper and his fireman jumped for their lives from the footplate. The unfortunate driver landed in the garden of the Arlesey sidings stationmaster's house (later renamed the Three Counties Sidings). He was killed instantly, along with his fireman who landed on the ballast on the other side of the train. The locomotive smashed into the goods wagons with such force that the tender was torn from the engine. Six of the carriages were completely wrecked.

One of the passengers on the train was a railway policeman by the name of Monk. He managed to scramble from the wreckage and go up to the signal box. Here he assisted the shocked signalman to warn approaching trains and telegraph for medical assistance and breakdown gangs. An even worse disaster was narrowly averted. The second half of the Manchester Express travelling at speed saw the Cadwell distant signals at danger and pulled up just short of the accident. Surgeons and nurses from surrounding areas soon arrived at the scene. Considering the damage to the train, they were surprised to find only three passengers had been killed, with 30 injured, some seriously. Some of the casualties were taken to Hitchin hospital on the Bedford Road. One of these was a seriously injured woman, Mrs Martha Burbridge. Because of her injuries her relatives arranged for her to recover at 40 Walsworth Road. Unfortunately, she never recovered sufficiently to return home, and died at no 40 in September 1909, 33 years after the accident!

Following the accident the Hitchin area became blocked with trains. At one point, seventeen trains tailed back from Hitchin towards Stevenage. The atmosphere at Hitchin station was subdued following the accident, but this changed to an atmosphere of surprise and amusement. Twelve elephants arrived at the station, having been released from their train in the backlog, and completed their journey on foot to a circus in town! It came to light at the inquiry into the crash that it was an accident waiting to happen. The first danger signal that Driver Pepper observed was only 898 yards ahead of the site of the derailment. Given a falling gradient of 1 in 230, a speed of 55 mph and greasy rails, the hand brake power on the locomotive, along with that of the guard's brake van, turned out to be woefully inadequate in their capacity to stop the train. It was recommended that the trains be fitted with a continuous brake, i.e. each coach having its own brakes operated from the engine by the driver.

MORE CASUALTIES

The parish records of Ickleford church show three individuals who died whilst servants of the railway, although the circumstances of their misfortune is not recorded. They are all interred in the churchyard, the first being George Jeeves who died on 9 November 1885. The second was John Irons, aged 42, who died on Boxing Day 1892. The third was George Underwood, aged 27 years, who died on 22 April 1893. George Jeeves' gravestone is still in the churchyard, near the wall facing the road. Part of the inscription, weathered with the passing of time, mentions his fellow workers at Hitchin, who probably contributed towards his stone.

MIDLAND MISHAP

A similar accident involving a train becoming derailed whilst crossing the main line occurred at Hitchin Station on Monday 3 September 1900. Fortunately, in this case there were no other trains approaching.

A five-coach train had arrived in the up platform from Bedford. Passengers alighted as the train terminated at Hitchin. When the all-clear was given, the train reversed back over the main line ready to return to Bedford. As it did so, the rear two coaches derailed on the points.

The signal box was informed immediately and all approaching trains were warned and stopped. The engine and the three intact coaches were moved away to a nearby siding and a breakdown gang was soon at work re-railing the two affected coaches. Once this had been done minor repairs were required on the track, and lines were reopened three hours later.

Although this incident caused no damage to life or limb it proved of great embarrassment to the Midland, having occurred on GNR territory, both still rival companies.

HUMAN TRAGEDY

Unfortunately, the railway has often provided a means for people to end their own lives. One of the most notable was that of a gentleman named Arthur Lucas of Winchester. He had shot himself on a Leeds to London express in October 1921. The express was stopped at Hitchin so that his body could be removed and an investigation carried out. His death was particularly poignant, as he was one of the survivors of the Titanic after she struck an iceberg in 1912.

The well-known Hitchin historian, Reginald Hine, also ended his life on the railway not long after the Second World War, in 1949.

HITCHIN'S MOST SPECTACULAR ACCIDENT

In more recent times a serious accident occurred on 19 November 1958 at Hitchin, near Benslow Bridge. Although fortunately there was no loss of life there was severe disruption to the railway system at Hitchin for nearly two days.

The time was 4.30am and there was dense fog. Three freight trains and a light engine were involved. A freight train from Ferme Park, London, to Peterborough slowed down approaching Hitchin South signal box to check the signals were clear, as they were difficult to see due to the fog. Another freight train, also travelling north, ran into the rear of the first train. This resulted in several goods wagons being derailed, blocking the railway completely. Almost at once, a freight train travelling south from Leeds ran into the wreckage. Its engine rolled onto its side with the impact, and many more wagons were strewn across all lines.

These piled up and fell onto a tank engine that had just left the locomotive shed. The engine was standing on the up slow line waiting to cross over to the station to collect its train. The crew of the engine, Driver Aitkins and Fireman Clarke, managed to climb out of the overturned locomotive and pick their way

The engine from which the Hitchin crew escaped in November 1958 lies on its side on the right, with wagons piled on top. (Bob Wheeler collection)

The loco of the second freight train going north has collided with the guard's van at the rear of the first train. Note the damage to the guard's van, caused by the impact from the goods wagon lying on its side. (Bob Wheeler collection)

The engine of the southbound freight from Leeds lies on its side, after running into the wreckage of the northbound trains. (John Toddington collection)

through the wreckage to safety. All of the crews involved were taken to hospital. Remarkably, none of the men was seriously injured.

The Hitchin breakdown crew was called out to the scene. The breakdown steam cranes from King's Cross and Peterborough were also summoned, their main task being to lift and re-rail the two overturned locomotives.

As all lines were completely blocked, and would be for some time, an emergency bus service was put into operation. Trains from King's Cross, with passengers travelling beyond Hitchin, were terminated at Stevenage. Buses were used to take them to Hitchin Station where they resumed their journeys either towards Peterborough or along the Hitchin to Cambridge branch.

At Peterborough, express trains travelling south were diverted to March, Ely, and Cambridge and into Liverpool Street station. Northbound express trains from King's Cross were cancelled or started from Peterborough.

The breakdown crews worked tirelessly to clear the wreckage, but the first line was not reopened until 5.45am, over 24 hours after the accident. All lines were cleared and track repaired just after 5am the following day.

The official report into the accident blamed the driver of the second freight travelling north for passing a stop signal at danger. His train then collided with the rear of the first train. The circumstances, however, were not in the driver's favour. He became confused where a colour light caution signal was beyond a first caution signal. This first caution signal was a semaphore signal with an oil lamp; the second was a yellow colour electric light.

The electric colour light signal, being so bright, overpowered the oil light signal causing him to "read through" the semaphore signal to the colour light beyond.

He was then further down the line than he realised, bearing in mind he was trying to stop a heavy express freight train. He then collided with the rear of the first train.

Since this accident Hitchin has only suffered minor derailments and incidents. Let's hope it stays this way, as the East Coast main line has had more than its share of accidents in recent years, at Hatfield (October 2000) and Potters Bar (May 2002), both resulting in tragic loss of life.

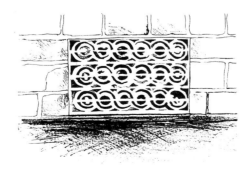

BRANCH LINE TRAINS
(CAUGHT AND MISSED)

THE HITCHIN TO CAMBRIDGE BRANCH

The Hitchin to Cambridge branch had a strange beginning, being only a part of a larger proposal. A bill for a railway, with Joseph Locke as engineer, was put before Parliament in 1845. It proposed a line to run from Oxford, through Thame, Aylesbury, Dunstable, Luton, Hitchin and on to Royston and Cambridge.

Parliament approved only the section of double track railway to run from Hitchin to Royston, 13 miles in length. This line was The Royston and Hitchin Railway, the bill receiving Royal assent on 16 July 1846.

The Great Northern Railway, under construction at that time from London to Peterborough, obtained authority to lease the line from the Royston and Hitchin as from 1 August 1850. The latter then applied to have the line extended to Cambridge, but this was refused. The following year they applied again and

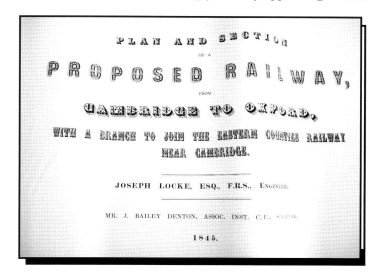

Title page of the prospectus for the Cambridge to Oxford Railway. (Hertfordshire Archives and Local Studies)

PLAN AND SECTION

OF A

PROPOSED RAILWAY,

FROM

CAMBRIDGE TO OXFORD,

WITH A BRANCH TO JOIN THE EASTERN COUNTIES RAILWAY
NEAR CAMBRIDGE.

JOSEPH LOCKE, ESQ., F.R.S., ENGINEER.

MR. J. BAILEY DENTON, ASSOC. INST. C. E., SURVEYOR.

1845.

this time were allowed to extend the line, but only as far as Shepreth. The line was opened in full from Hitchin to Shepreth in August 1851. As GNR trains had to terminate at Shepreth, they arranged to connect with Cambridge by using horse-drawn omnibuses.

A rival company, the Eastern Counties Railway, then came on the scene. It had constructed and was running a line from Bishopsgate (London) to Cambridge. This company agreed a truce with the GNR and, between them, they agreed to build a single line south from Cambridge to Shepreth. This opened in April 1852, joining up with the original railway. The horse omnibus service from Shepreth to Cambridge became redundant and was thus withdrawn.

The Eastern Counties Railway was then granted a lease by the GNR for 14 years to work the line to Hitchin until 1866. The GNR was not happy with this scheme, however, and wanted to work its own through trains between London and Cambridge. The two companies reached a compromise, with the Great Eastern Railway (which had in 1862 taken over the ECR) agreeing to double the line from Cambridge to Shepreth. This work was completed and ready for traffic by 31 March 1866. Thus the GNR was able to run its own trains directly from King's Cross to Cambridge, the distance from Hitchin to Cambridge being 26 miles.

SOME STATIONS ALONG THE BRANCH
LETCHWORTH

The first Letchworth station, a small halt, was built in 1903 for the new Garden City which was founded in the same year. Two years later in 1905 a larger, but temporary, station was constructed. A permanent station was built nearer to the town centre in 1912/13, as the First Garden City grew. Two island platforms were built, intended for four tracks, but only two were provided. There was an extensive goods yard on the Cambridge (down) side of the line, and a large goods

The site of the crossing gates where the line crossed Works Road. A crossing gate post can be seen in the centre of the picture, taken in May 2005. (Author)

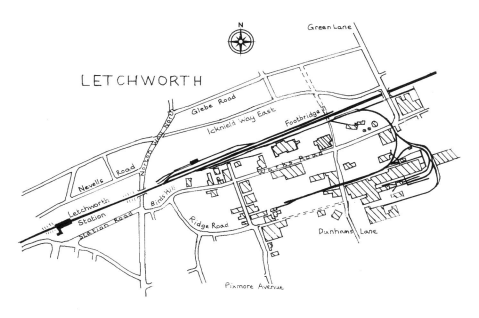

A diagram of the Letchworth industrial branch line, based on an original in the possession of the Letchworth Heritage Museum. Crossing gates were provided where the line crossed Green Lane, Works Road and Dunhams Lane. (Zena Grant)

shed. On the London (up) side of the line, a short siding went behind the up platform. Any livestock that arrived was unloaded onto this platform into pens before collection by local farmers and butchers. The author recalls a rare event in the 1950s when, with his father, he watched a circus train arrive at the siding one Saturday morning. Elephants, a few giraffes and various other circus animals were unloaded from the train and walked in a procession up Eastcheap to a large circus tent that was erected on the green opposite the fire station, much to the amusement of many shoppers. This green is now the Arena car park.

Letchworth was well known for the many industries in its large factory area. Much of the parcel traffic handled in the goods yard consisted of paper and punch cards for the International Computer and Tabulating Company (ICT) which later became more famous as International Computers Limited (ICL). The company had several factories and employed thousands of people from Letchworth and the surrounding area. Many other industries were served by a single-track railway that branched off the main line, and started on the up side, near the station. The first location on the line was the power station. Many coal trucks were stabled at the power station to provide coal for the making of electricity for the town. The line then continued ahead and split into two. The top half of the line continued ahead and crossed Green Lane over a level crossing to serve the Letchworth Bacon Company and a timber works. The other part of the line veered off to the right into the gas works and, via a level crossing, over Works Road into the K&L Steelworks.

There were several sidings in the steel works that accommodated many wagons loaded with steel to be distributed to various parts of the country. The line then continued, over yet another level crossing, this time over Dunham's Lane, into Meridew's furniture factory.

Such was the number of wagons to be shunted on this branch line that a shunting engine came to Letchworth from Hitchin and spent most of the day shunting at the various industries mentioned.

A diesel shunting loco on the industrial branch at Letchworth in September 1966. The factory roof in the background is K&L Steelworks. (John Toddington collection)

With the demise of local manufacturing industries in the early 1970s the branch became less and less used and was closed in the late 1970s when demand for its use ceased.

Letchworth soon came back into the limelight with the transformation from diesel to electric power in 1978. Several sidings were built on the down side to accommodate electric multiple unit (EMU) trains that worked trains from the branch into King's Cross and Moorgate. A train-washing plant was installed, and raised platforms were provided alongside the trains to allow access for cleaners and railway staff to board the trains.

Apart from the King's Cross-Cambridge trains that pass through

Letchworth, there is a basic hourly service from Letchworth to Moorgate which travels via the Hertford branch.

BALDOCK

Baldock was the main stabling point for outer suburban trains, which were kept overnight in sidings on the down side. There was also a small goods yard on the down side, and a siding into Larkinson's scrap yard. On the up side a siding served a goods shed, the main goods traffic being lingerie from the Kayser Bondor Company.

This company had a large production works in the High Street. A Tesco Supermarket has since been built on the site which incorporates the original façade, though the rest of the works has been demolished.

Also on the up side, the siding served a large maltings. This was a typically-shaped maltings building, and was a familiar landmark to travellers on the railway and the adjacent Royston Road (A505) until it burnt down in the early 1990s. These buildings were used for many of the outdoor sequences in Ronnie Barker's TV series "Porridge".

At the end of the down platform was Baldock signal box which was the only box on the branch open 24 hours a day. This was to ensure the sidings were available round the clock for commuter train stabling. The station itself was unique as it was the only station on the branch to have its platforms connected by a subway.

ASHWELL & MORDEN

As the name implies Ashwell station serves not only the village of Ashwell, but also the two villages of Guilden Morden and Steeple Morden which are just over the Hertfordshire border in Cambridgeshire; the station is in fact in Odsey, and a considerable distance from all three!

The station has been famous over the years for winning the best kept station award on several occasions. Its flower gardens were a joy to behold in the summertime, thanks to the hard work and dedication of the station staff.

The location of the station was a bugbear for train crews, especially in steam days. As trains left the up platform towards London, they had to tackle an incline through a cutting which had steep sides, with many overhanging trees.

In the autumn months the track sometimes became covered in leaves, and locomotives had difficulty starting away from the station. Their wheels slipped profusely, and sand had to be applied to the track from the locomotives' sand boxes before they could get adhesion and manage to start away up the cutting. In more modern times, despite its isolated location, the station has a large number of commuters using its trains.

Today, the road leading away from the station towards Ashwell is lined on both sides by parked cars for several hundred yards, as the station has only a small car park.

ROYSTON

From 1977, Royston, 44 miles from King's Cross, was the outermost station of the GN outer suburban service, until the line from Royston to Cambridge was electrified in the 1980s. In its heyday, Royston had an extensive goods yard which included eight private sidings. Some of the goods handled included large amounts of barley, which were loaded into bulk container wagons to form a complete train.

These trains of barley were dispatched to Scotland for processing in the whisky industry. Other freight handled included racehorses from local racing stables, pigs and fertiliser. Often, a goods wagon was put on a siding that went behind the signal box on the up side to be loaded with lampshades from BTD, the lampshade factory in York Way.

In 1962, the station handled 138,000 tons of goods, which gives an idea of how busy the station was. In more recent times, two trains a day of petrol tankers served a Shell petrol distribution site on the down side.

Today these trains no longer run, and Royston is now like the other stations on the line, providing a fast and efficient passenger service between London and Cambridge. The goods side of the railway has slipped into an almost-forgotten bygone age.

THE THREE COUNTIES HOSPITAL TRAMWAY

The Three Counties Hospital was between Arlesey and Stotfold, four miles north of Hitchin. A site (now a residential development) was chosen in the mid-nineteenth century to build an "asylum" for the treatment of the mentally ill, this venture being funded by three neighbouring counties, Bedfordshire, Hertfordshire and Huntingdonshire who at this time had overcrowded facilities for such patients.

In 1853 these counties agreed to share the cost of constructing and running a new hospital, which was aptly named Three Counties, in later years renamed Fairfield hospital.

It was decided to build a tramway from the Great Northern main line to the site of the hospital. The tramway was laid first so that it could convey all the building materials required for the vast hospital complex. Railway sidings were purchased from the Arlesey Cement Company adjacent to the main railway.

The tramway started at the cement works sidings, ran into Station Road, over the Arlesey to Hitchin road and alongside the drive up to the hospital. It was in total just over a mile in length.

The line was in use for more than two years before the hospital was ready for opening.

After the hospital opened in late 1859 the tramway was used to transport coal and other supplies to various parts of the hospital. Presumably the line closed when motor transport became a more popular way of transporting materials.

The tramway passed through this arch to a small station beyond. Photograph 1999. (Author)

There is no trace of the line along its route today except in the hospital itself in the walled yard near the former laundry, and an arch remains where the line went into a small station with a short platform with wooden buffers. The hospital closed in 1998, taking with it yet another railway memory from the past.

ARLESEY CEMENT WORKS TRAMWAY (BLUE LAGOON NARROW GAUGE RAILWAY)

Just south of the Three Counties Tramway, and running parallel to it, was another line, built to service the cement works of the Arlesey Brick and Lime Company. The works came into operation in 1858, and were supplied with chalk by means of a narrow gauge tramway from a large quarry about half a mile away. The chalk was processed in the cement works, and was used to make lime and cement. In 1930 the quarry started to flood. By 1932, it became unworkable, resulting in the closure of the tramway and the cement works. The flooded quarry still exists, and is known locally as the Blue Lagoon, where sailing and fishing are enjoyed.

ANOTHER LINE TO LONDON?

In 1861, a group of speculators proposed a line to run from the Midland at Hitchin to London via Codicote and St Albans, by-passing the Great Northern, and allowing the Midland an independent route into London. The proposal included a junction with the Metropolitan, London's first underground railway, which was then being built between Paddington and Aldersgate (now Barbican) stations.

The London & Midland Junction Railway, had it been built, would have had a considerable effect on the Highbury area of Hitchin, with a deep cutting as shown in the map on p65. Perhaps not surprisingly, this project never got beyond the drawing board, but it is interesting to speculate what an important junction Hitchin would have been if this railway had been built instead of the eventual Midland main line from St Pancras, through Luton, direct to Bedford and beyond.

HITCHIN WESTERN RAILWAY

Scores of proposals were made in the early days of the railways to promote and build new lines; many succeeded but a large number failed. Two notable failures were connected with the Hitchin area. The first was to be called the Hitchin Western Railway, which was proposed in 1889. A well-known Hitchin man, George Beaver, was a railway surveyor by profession. He was one of the first railway surveyors to find work in the early days of the railways. It was only natural for him to become involved in the proposals, being a local man.

It was intended to build a line five miles and five furlongs long from Hitchin via Great Offley terminating at Lilley. The line was to leave Hitchin and pass the Maydencroft Estate. The Victorian engineers then faced a major challenge.

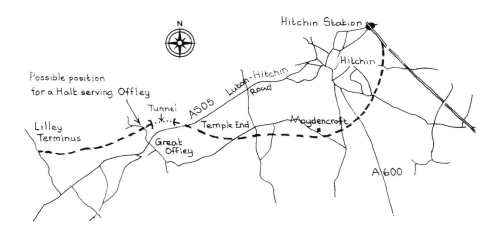

Route of the proposed railway between Hitchin and Lilley. (Zena Grant)

Above: Proposed route of the London & Midland Junction Railway, showing the junction with the Midland, just north of Nightingale Road. (Hertfordshire Archives & Local Studies)

Left: Front page of the prospectus for the London & Midland Junction Railway (Hertfordshire Archives and Local Studies)

They proposed a tunnel through Offley Hill which would have to be 1,127 yards in length. This tunnel would have been a massive project to complete even though the hill was made of chalk. The line was to come out of the tunnel in the vicinity of Offley windmill. Once the line had left Offley it was to continue on to Lilley. A terminus station was to be built near Lilley village centre.

There were objections to the line from local landowners, and the Offley tunnel was realistically too ambitious a scheme. The final blow to the proposals came when the business community of Luton was approached for financial assistance. For reasons unknown they failed to come up with sufficient funds to extend the line on to Luton.

LEIGHTON BUZZARD & HITCHIN RAILWAY

The second line was proposed by three gentlemen from the neighbouring county of Bedfordshire. They were William Smith Cowper-Cooper who resided at Toddington Manor, John Wough of Toddington, a surgeon, and Henry J Green, of Leighton Buzzard, a maltster. These men proposed a cross-country route to run from the London and North Western Railway at Leighton Buzzard across to the Midland Railway at Ickleford, just north of Hitchin. They applied to Parliament in 1899, under the Light Railway Act, 1896.

During the next three years the proposers surveyed the route and canvassed for financial support. The estimated cost was to be £100,000, the line 19½ miles long. Some of the clauses in the application were that the line be a single line, its construction to be completed in five years, and steam power only to be used. The fares were to be 1st class: 3d per mile; 2nd class: 2d per mile; and 3rd class 1d per mile.

The stations the line would serve and their mileages from Leighton Buzzard were:

Hockcliffe 5 miles;
Toddington 7 miles;
Harlington 9 miles;
Barton-Le-Clay 13 miles;
Shillington 16 miles;
Ickleford 19 miles, where it
would join the Midland Railway
and run into Hitchin.

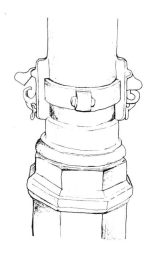

Unfortunately, as was the case with many other railway proposals, the difficulty was raising sufficient funds, so the scheme was abandoned. Some earthworks were started in Barton Cutting, but halted when the proposal failed.

MIXED GOODS

THE FESTIVAL OF BRITAIN HITCHIN PAGEANT: "THE FIRST TRAIN"

This pageant was held from Monday 28 May to Saturday 2 June 1951, with performances every evening and on Saturday afternoon. The then Queen (later Her Majesty the Queen Mother) attended on the Monday. One of the main events of the pageant was a celebration of the coming of the railway to Hitchin just over 100 years previously.

The Hitchin Model Engineering Club played a major role in this event, carrying out a great deal of research to ensure authenticity.

A train was built in a barn in the grounds of Hitchin Priory. A group of club members met on Saturday afternoons to convert a Fordson tractor and trailer into the "locomotive". Two farm trailers were converted into "carriages". The Priory locomotive and train were intended for an enactment of the first train to enter Hitchin in 1850. The track for the train consisted of a single circuit of the road around Priory Park. All the public were in the centre, so only the visible half of the train was completed and painted. Many onlookers dressed in period costume of the mid-nineteenth century to add atmosphere to the event. Her Majesty the Queen was escorted by Mr F. Foster, Chairman of Hitchin Urban District Council. They watched eagerly as the train came into view, belching real smoke and blowing its steam whistle. The Queen joined in the applause as the train passed, and shared in the laughter when, as at the actual event in 1850, the rear coach broke away from the train.

CABBIES' SHELTER – THE RESTORATION PROJECT

Earlier in the book, we learned about the origins of the little wooden cabbies' hut, funded by the generosity of local commuters, and captured as background to the photograph of station staff around 1903. It was a relic of the days when the working cabbie, originally with a horse-drawn vehicle, had to wait in all weathers outside the station.

Local memories still exist of its open door and gas-lit interior, and of cabbies downing steaming "cuppas" between fares. The hut later became home to the car park attendant; hospitality still flourished, and a telephone was added to its conveniences. But cab technology advanced as did the need for more space on the station forecourt. Heaters and radios became standard features in taxis, enabling the driver to sit tight in his vehicle. Pressure for more parking space increased.

By the early 1970s the hut was beginning to look derelict. The planned forecourt changes rendered it obsolete. John Myatt was a local resident whose affection for the shelter went back to his student days. By now he was married and living in Radcliffe Road. He contacted the Station Master and offered to buy it as it stood for an agreed price of £60 plus Purchase Tax.

After some convoluted negotiations, the Myatt family became proud custodians of the shelter. In 1976, a team of local volunteers using a Land Rover and trailer transported the purchase to their back garden, where it was to be transformed into a summer house.

John Myatt and friends move the shelter from the station forecourt in 1976. (Alan Millard)

It was there that Hitchin Historical Society members discovered it, quite by chance, in the summer of 1997. Time and circumstances had intervened, and the summer house project had never come to fruition.

The little wooden hut was gently rotting away. Appreciating that they owned a fascinating relic of local railway history, John and Patsy Myatt generously offered the structure to the town.

Keith Hoskins, Town Centre Manager, was "on board" from the beginning and, under his guidance, possible sites and uses for a restored hut were considered. Market Place and Community Kiosk were quickly decided on, and everyone worked to that end.

The seventeen-month restoration project, during which Society Chairman Scilla Douglas enthused, cajoled, organised and harnessed energies, grew into a remarkable community venture. Although the basic structure was sound, it soon became apparent just how much work would be needed. Portions of the woodwork had rotted, in particular the base and around the porch, and the roof and glazing needed serious attention.

'Raising the roof' in Hitchin Market Place, 22 September 1998. (Scilla Douglas)

Volunteers worked hundreds of hours and local firms provided expertise, labour, materials and services such as storage and transport free of charge. National bodies advised and encouraged. All this endeavour bore fruit on Saturday 10 October 1998 when, on Grand Cabbies' Day, the shelter was officially welcomed to Hitchin Market Place and "adopted" by North Herts. District Council.

GNR 150 YEAR ANNIVERSARY

The railway at Hitchin celebrated its 150th birthday in August 2000. To mark this historic anniversary, several events were organised.

Hitchin Museum presented a major exhibition called "Back Tracking", which ran from 8 July to 27 August. The exhibition looked at "railway mania" in the 19th century, the development and building of the railway line, and the effect

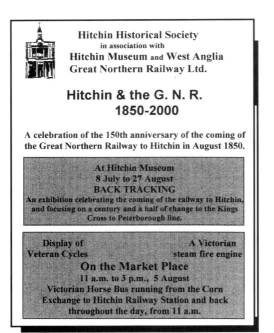

A programme produced by the Hitchin Historical Society announcing events to celebrate the 150th anniversary of the coming of the railway to Hitchin. (Hitchin Historical Society)

A selection of signs and nameplates at Hitchin Museum in the 'Back Tracking' 150-year anniversary display. (Scilla Douglas)

it has had on the town from 1850 to the present day. Many railway exhibits of the era were on display, including items borrowed from the National Railway Museum. Among these were original station name plates, oil lamps and various photographs and track plans from over the years. As part of the GNR 150 celebrations, Hitchin held a festival of various events, which included a walk organised by the Hitchin Historical Society. The walk was held on Sunday 9 July and the guide was a local historian and Society member David Howlett. The walk started at the booking hall in the station and took in various buildings and landmarks associated with the railway and ended at the museum in Paynes Park. A modified form of this walk has been repeated regularly as part of the Hitchin Festival, and a walk leaflet is available locally.

The largest event took place on Saturday 5 August and was organised by Hitchin Historical Society in association with Hitchin Museum and West Anglia Great Northern Railway Ltd (WAGN). A genuine 1897 London General Omnibus Company horse bus ran a service from the Corn Exchange to the station and back. The bus was operated by Tony Drewitt of Epsom, who is well-

The horse-drawn bus outside the Corn Exchange, with self-explanatory display boards. Hitchin Museum curator Gillian Riding in period costume, and Hitchin Historical Society member David Howlett in GNR stationmaster's uniform. (Scilla Douglas)

Members of Hitchin Historical Society outside the Corn Exchange in period dress – and a few modern-day bystanders as well! (Scilla Douglas)

known for the ownership of the vehicle and attends various events throughout the country.

The first passengers to use the bus were a group of members of the Royston Historical Society who travelled to Hitchin by train. They were in period costume and were given free tickets for the train, courtesy of WAGN. They boarded the bus at the station and were met on arrival at the Corn Exchange by Councillor Judi Billing, Chairman of the NHDC Hitchin Committee; Keith Hoskins, Town Centre Manager; Gillian Riding, Hitchin Museum curator; and members of Hitchin Historical Society.

The bus provided a splendid sight outside the Corn Exchange and was surrounded by various artefacts of the time. They included vintage bicycles and trade cycles, a tinker's cart and a chimney sweep's cycle. Also close by was a Shand Mason Victorian steam fire engine of 1876 owned by Derek Wheeler of Hitchin, a retired school teacher and well-known local historian. Many photographs where taken of this impressive gathering by the public and local press, and will be looked upon in future to remind us of this splendid occasion.

A CURIOUS FIND

Not far from Ickleford, near Hitchin, a plateway still exists, now mostly hidden below soil on a track running up a steep incline towards nearby fields. It was constructed by a local farmer in the 1920s, at a time when sidings at Hitchin were becoming blocked with train loads of manure from London. A siding off the Great Northern main line was built near Ickleford, and horses and carts would collect the manure from the trains and take it up the incline to manure "clamps" ready to be spread on the fields. It soon became muddy in wet weather and, due to the steepness of the incline, it became difficult to pull the carts up the track. The plateway was the ingenious solution to this problem.

The plateway rails were made of iron, each about 7" wide, set in concrete, and laid to fit the width of the cart wheels, which were something over four feet wide. There is a small raised edge on the inside of each rail to stop the cart wheels slipping off. Plateways as modern as this are quite unusual. In the days before railways as we know them today, in the late eighteenth and early nineteenth centuries, plateways were sometimes built in industrial locations such as collieries.

The author recalls in his boyhood days trainspotting at this location. He and his friends took it in turns to ride their cycles down one of the tracks to see who could stay on to the bottom. Nearly everyone came off the plateway and ended up in the hedge alongside!

THE HITCHIN AND DISTRICT MODEL ENGINEERING CLUB

The Hitchin Pageant in 1951 would not have been possible but for the involvement of the Hitchin and District Model Engineering Club. The club had

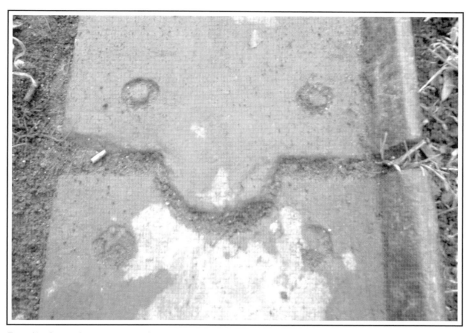

Detail of the plateway, showing a rail joint. Photograph June 2006. (Phil Rowe)

A view of the plateway, looking up the incline. The raised inner edges can be plainly seen. Photograph June 2006. (Simon Walker)

its headquarters in a large shed adjacent to the railway bridge in Grove Road, Hitchin. A plain oval of elevated track 440ft long, of 3½inch and 5inch gauges, was constructed. This allowed members to try out locomotives they had built, with other model engineering clubs being invited at times to come along to Hitchin to use the track. The author recalls in the late 1950s, whilst train spotting on a Saturday at Hitchin station, word getting around that steam model engines were in use at Grove Road. Several of us then walked to Grove Road and after a patient wait were invited to ride around the track being pulled by one of the model locomotives – what a great way to spend a Saturday!

The club moved from the site in 1985, and the track was dismantled. The Hitchin and District Model Engineering Club has since been reformed as the Hitchin Society of Model Engineers which still has an active membership. Some members still construct locomotives from scratch and run them on an oval track in the garden of a member's private house.

A member from a visiting club drives a locomotive around the Grove Road track in the 1950s. A smoke deflector tube in the loco's chimney is to keep the smoke away from the driver. (John Scorer collection)

The author at the controls of a locomotive with Keith Wilson, secretary of the Hitchin &
District Model Engineering Club. Summer 2003. (John Scorer collection)

RECENT AND FUTURE DEPARTURES

The main change noted at Hitchin in the late 1990s was the remodelling of the station approach and forecourt. Several bus stands have been provided on the station forecourt alongside an extended taxi rank. The bus stands are a definite improvement on the previous arrangement. Buses previously stopped outside the Station Approach, in Walsworth Road, sometimes causing traffic build-up. Buses now arrive on the station forecourt, making for a much easier interchange between road and rail passenger transport.

During the clearing of the ground for the reconstruction of the forecourt contractors came across several lengths of track buried beneath the tarmac. These were the remains of a siding that served sheep and cattle pens opposite the station entrance. The contractors were instructed not to disturb the footpath outside the booking hall as there are a few drain covers and other items that bear the GNR insignia which, thanks to this forethought, are still in place today.

Unfortunately, there were some casualties in the clearing of the yard, namely some ancient horse-chestnut trees that probably dated back to the opening of the railway in 1850. Representation to leave the trees in situ was made to the local authority, but retention of the trees was not part of the plan, and they were felled to help make better use of the forecourt. These have, however, been replaced with two young horse chestnuts.

FUTURE MODERNISATION

As far as track layout is concerned, passengers travelling round the branch line to Letchworth, Royston and beyond to Cambridge are often delayed whilst their train waits to cross over the main line onto the Cambridge branch. An upgrade to the East Coast main line has been proposed, and one of the features is a flyover, crossing the main line at Hitchin onto the Cambridge branch. This would alleviate delay and would be a safer proposition for passengers and create a safer layout at this busy rail junction. Unfortunately this project has been shelved by the Strategic Rail Authority. The Authority has withdrawn this scheme from its Rail Passenger Partnership funding - a system that allows local authorities to bid for money to carry out improvement work. The reason for withdrawing this funding scheme is not known, but it also means a proposal to extend the platforms at Letchworth station and to re-install working lifts has also been shelved until around 2008.

Another project that would have improved rail services in the area was to extend the Thameslink service to Hitchin and beyond to Peterborough and Cambridge. The project would have opened new direct journey options to places such as Gatwick and Brighton. This project (originally known as "Thameslink 2000") has been delayed many times. At long last, however, there may be some light at the end of the tunnel. In 2006, the government finally gave authority for a new St Pancras Thameslink station to be built under the almost complete St Pancras International station. As part of these works, well under way at the time of writing, a link railway is to be built to this new station from the Great Northern line between Finsbury Park and King's Cross. With both Thameslink and Great Northern services run by First Capital Connect, it is to be hoped that direct trains from Hitchin to Gatwick and Brighton may not be far away.

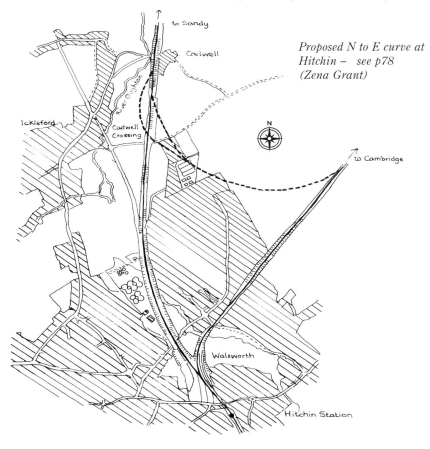

Proposed N to E curve at Hitchin – see p78 (Zena Grant)

What else does the future hold? Who knows? The two decaying goods sheds in Nightingale Road converted into luxury flats?

A more ambitious plan, to revive the old cross-country route from Cambridge to Oxford, was to have involved Hitchin. Like many proposed routes since railways began, this particular scheme failed due to lack of finance. The plan was to run trains along the existing line from Cambridge, via Royston to Hitchin, then on to Sandy (the original London & North Western Railway line which ran from Cambridge direct to Sandy via Gamlingay and Potton was closed in 1968 and subsequently removed). It was proposed to build a brand-new east-to-north curve just north of Hitchin station, allowing trains from Letchworth to proceed direct towards Arlesey, and beyond, to Sandy. The main expense would then involve relaying the line from Sandy to Bedford. This old line passed through the stations of Blunham and Willington. The line from Bedford to Oxford is still in use today, so the line from Sandy to Bedford is the only section requiring relaying to complete the original line. After six years of planning, these plans were put to the Strategic Rail Authority (SRA) in 2001, but were turned down due to a lack of funding. The scheme was to have cost £240 million, and was expected to have created up to 10,000 jobs, but the SRA claimed that there was little cash left after the Hatfield disaster in October 2000.

In April 2006, WAGN lost the passenger franchise for Great Northern services between King's Cross and Peterborough and Cambridge, including the Hertford Loop. First Capital Connect, part of the First Group of companies, has promised great things, but it is probably too early to say what effect its takeover will have on the ordinary passenger.

In June, 2006, while this book was being prepared for press, news emerged that Hitchin is likely to retain the transhipment facility for roadstone that it had seen during the building of the nearby Baldock bypass road. It is also expected that a service of regular scrap steel trains will run from Hitchin to south Wales. Both these services will be operated by Freightliner.

Hitchin Station office doors. (Caroline

Whatever the outcome, Hitchin once boasted two steam sheds, two branch lines and two main lines, not bad for a small market town. There are still a few reminders of the past in and around the station. Let's hope they remain to remind future generations of how the railway really was. Hopefully this book will also provide a window into the past.

ROAD NAMES OFF ST MICHAEL'S ROAD

Each road name has a railway theme, as the estate is built on the site of the old Railway stockyard.

CUBITT CLOSE

(Sir) William Cubitt (1785-1861) was a talented civil engineer who built several railways including the Great Northern Railway as its consulting engineer from 1844-1855. Sir William also supervised the erection of the famous London landmark, Crystal Palace, in 1851, for which he was knighted. His brother, Benjamin, was also the company's first Locomotive Superintendent.

HOLDEN CLOSE

James Holden (1837-1925) rose through the ranks of several railway companies until he became Locomotive Superintendent of the Great Eastern Railway in 1865. Whilst with this company he developed the design of several steam locomotives, his most famous being the "Claud Hamilton" type. Holden also built a 0-10-0 well-tank locomotive, known as the "Decapod". This was designed to rival the then emerging electric motive power. The locomotive was very powerful, being designed to accelerate a load of 300 tons to 30mph in 30 seconds. It turned out to be too heavy to be useful on regular services and was soon converted to a more conventional wheel arrangement. Holden also pioneered experiments in the use of oil as a fuel for locomotives as a substitute for coal. He was a Quaker and had built London's first hostel for railwaymen in 1890. He retired in 1907 and was succeeded by his son S.D. Holden, who held the post until 1912.

IVATT CLOSE

Henry Alfred Ivatt (1851-1923) started his railway career at Crewe Locomotive works, and gained practical experience as a fireman on trains operating out of Crewe. He rose through management ranks and moved to Ireland in 1877 where he became Chief Locomotive Engineer of The Great Southern and Western

Railway of Ireland. He moved back to England in 1895, and became Chief Locomotive Superintendent of the Great Northern Railway. At this time there was a large increase of traffic on the railways. Ivatt set about designing more powerful engines to handle this increase, achieving this with larger boilers and grate areas. Probably the most famous of the locomotives he designed were the "Ivatt Atlantics" which served their purpose well for many years. Ivatt retired in 1911, and died in 1923 at his home in Sussex.

MERMAID CLOSE

A "Mermaid" was the name given to a type of wagon used on engineering trains. These wagons had a side tilting body to enable their contents – usually ballast – to be tipped at the side of the track.

NIMBUS WAY

"Nimbus" was the name of a "Deltic" class diesel locomotive of 3,300 horsepower. These locomotives were the principal class to take over from steam the haulage of express trains on the East Coast main line that runs through Hitchin. Nimbus was famous for hauling the Flying Scotsman train in a time of six hours from Kings Cross to Edinburgh in June 1962. Named, like several of the "Deltics", after a racehorse (Nimbus won the Derby in 1949) this particular loco was delivered to BR in 1962, and was finally withdrawn from service in 1979.

PEPPERCORN WALK

Arthur H. Peppercorn (1889-1951) began his railway career in 1905 with the Great Northern Railway. He progressed through the ranks and became Chief Mechanical Engineer of the London and North Eastern Railway in 1946, a post he retained until 1949, after nationalisation.

Peppercorn was best known for his design of the very successful class "A1"and "A2" pacific locomotives which were a common sight hauling express trains through Hitchin from the 1940s until the end of the steam era. One of these locomotives was named "A H Peppercorn", after its designer. Built just before Nationalisation, the tender briefly carried the letters "LNER", before the change to "British Railways".

PULLMAN DRIVE

Named after George Mortimer Pullman (1831-1897) an American who invented the "Pullman" carriage. These carriages formed trains that had a luxury interior arranged as lounge and restaurant cars. In the United Kingdom, the Midland Railway Company was first to adopt Pullman cars, in 1873.

Six years later, the Great Northern Railway inaugurated a Pullman dining service which worked out of King's Cross. By 1939, there were 58 Pullman cars on the London & North Eastern Railway, but the service had to be suspended for the duration of the war. Some preserved Pullman cars are still in use today, and the name "Pullman" is still used for a small number of express trains that run through Hitchin.

STIRLING CLOSE
Patrick Stirling (1820-1895) was born in Scotland, and served several Scottish railway companies before he moved to the Great Northern Railway in 1866. In these early pioneering days of the GNR, Stirling designed and had built several classes of locomotive. They were designed for power and speed to tackle some of the continuous gradients on the York – London main line. Probably his most famous class of locomotive was the "Stirling Single" which had two eight foot driving wheels. One of these locomotives, No.1 (mentioned in chapter 4) is preserved in its original condition (albeit paired with an incorrect tender) in the National Railway Museum at York.

STURROCK WAY
Archibald Sturrock (1816-1909) was born in Scotland, where he worked for several railway companies in the early part of his career. He went to the Great Western Railway in 1840 and then transferred to the Great Northern Railway as its Locomotive Superintendent from 1850 until 1866. He promoted several ideas for designs of steam locomotives, some of which did not meet with the company directors' approval. In 1863, one of his inventions was the steam tender.

This tender ran on six coupled wheels, and was designed as an additional source of power at low speeds when the locomotive was starting off with a heavy train. It was not popular with enginemen, as it was heavy on steam and caused them extra work. The shareholders of the company were not amused with the cost of his invention, and he left the company on early retirement at the age of fifty. He retired to live the life of a country squire, this lifestyle obviously suiting him as it lasted 43 years until he died in 1909, aged 92.

TALISMAN STREET
"The Talisman" was the name of a titled express train that ran through Hitchin, and in later years actually stopped there. Its first run was in September 1956 from King's Cross to Edinburgh. The train was very popular, taking only 6hrs.40mins to reach Edinburgh – very fast for the time. The train saw out steam haulage and became diesel hauled usually by 3,300hp "Deltic" locomotives. In 1964 a Hitchin stop was added to the "Talisman" timetable. There were two trains a day, one in each direction. The northbound train stopped at Hitchin in the morning and the southbound one in the afternoon. This pattern continued until 1968 when the title was removed from the timetable. In the 1970s, the name was again introduced for the 4pm departure from Edinburgh and King's Cross. The name finally disappeared from the timetable in the late 1980s.

WEDGEWOOD CLOSE

Sir Ralph Lewis Wedgwood (1875-1956) – the road name is a misspelling – rose rapidly through the North Eastern Railway ranks. He became Company Secretary at age 30, then Chief Goods Manager at 36. After the First World War he became Deputy General Manager of the Company. He then became Chief General Manager when the above Company formed part of the London and North Eastern Railway in the "Grouping" of 1923. He was knighted in 1924, and continued his career until he retired in 1942, having had an A4 Pacific locomotive named after him. He died in 1956.

WORSDELL WAY

Thomas William Worsdell (1838-1916) started his railway career at Crewe but went to America for six years where he became Master Mechanic at the Pennsylvania Railroad's famous Altoona Works. He returned to Crewe in 1871, then in 1885 he was offered and accepted the post of Locomotive Superintendent with the North Eastern Railway. He designed several types of steam locomotive that became the basis of NER designs for the next twenty to thirty years. He retired in 1890 due to ill health and was replaced by his brother Wilson Worsdell, who was Assistant Mechanical Engineer at the time; he held the post until 1910. Thomas died in 1916.

Hitchin Station in the late 1950s, gas lamps still in situ. A tank engine waits at the up platform, while two engines steam gently in the shed. A down freight has stopped at the original gantry. (Anonymous donor)

SELECTIVE GLOSSARY

ASHPITS
Location, in an engine shed, where the remains of the fire was dropped at the end of the working day – not a pleasant job.

AUTOMATIC WARNING SYSTEM (AWS)
System for alerting the driver to a signal aspect which requires action.

A horn sounds for caution (yellow) or danger (red) with a bell indicating a clear (green) signal ahead. If the horn is not cancelled, after a short interval, the brakes are automatically applied.

GRATE AREA
The area on the surface of the grate on which coal lies in the firebox. The greater the grate area, the more heat there is available to produce steam.

GROUPING
Under an act of parliament passed in 1921, most of the railway companies of Great Britain were formed, on 1 January 1923, into what became known as the "Big Four". These were the Great Western Railway, the Southern Railway, the London Midland & Scottish Railway and the London & North Eastern Railway.

LEVER FRAME
The levers, and associated rodding underneath them, in a signalbox. Small frames were sometimes in a smaller cabin, or even out in the open.

SIGNALS (SLOTTED AND SOMERSAULT)
Early railway signals came in all sorts of shapes, sizes and colours. Gradually, the use of an arm, raised or lowered to show clear, or horizontal to show caution or danger, became standard.

In the early days of the GNR, slotted signalposts were used in which the signal fitted inside the post when not showing danger.

With hindsight, it is clear that such an arrangement was not terribly safe (see chapter 3) and the centre-balanced "somersault" signals, designed by Hitchin signalling inspector Edward French, became standard on the company's lines.

SINGLE
See "Wheel arrangement"

TRAIN LOG (OR REGISTER)
The book kept in a signalbox to record all train movements and other activity associated with the passing of trains through the section of line for which the signalman is responsible.

WELL-TANK (AND OTHER TYPES OF TANK LOCOMOTIVE)
Express steam locomotives generally had a separate tender behind the locomotive to carry the coal and water needed on the journey. Tank engines had no tender, the coal being carried in a "bunker" at the rear of the cab, and the water in an integral tank. The position of the water tank determined whether the engine was known as a pannier, saddle, side or well tank engine.

WHEEL ARRANGEMENT
A method (sometimes known as the Whyte Notation after its American inventor, F.W. Whyte) of denoting the arrangement of wheels on a steam locomotive. There are normally three numbers, e.g. "4-6-2" denotes four leading wheels, followed by six driving wheels and finally two trailing wheels. If there was just one pair of driving wheels (common in nineteenth century express passenger locomotives) it was known as a "single" with a wheel arrangement perhaps 2-2-2 or 4-2-2.

WHEELTAPPING
A method of testing the integrity of a wheel on a railway coach or wagon by hitting it with a special hammer. An expert ear can detect flaws in the wheel. Ultrasonic methods of routine testing have rendered wheeltapping redundant.

SOURCES

Bonavia M.R.	The Cambridge Line	Ian Allen 1995
Cockman F.G.	The Railways of Hertfordshire	Hertfordshire Library Service 1978
Curtis G.	A Chronicle of Small Beer	Phillimore 1970
Davies R. & Grant M.D.	Forgotten Railways Chilterns & Cotswolds	David & Charles 1975
Douglas P. & Humphries P.	Discovering Hitchin	Egon Publishers 1995
Douglas P. & Humphries P.	The Hitchin Cabmen's Shelter	A Hitchin Historical Society Publication 1998
Gordon W.J.	Our Home Railways	Frederick Warne & Co. 1910
Hodge P.	The Hertford Loop	Southgate Civic Trust 1976
Latchmore E.A.	People Places and Past Times of Hitchin	
Milligan E.H.	Quakers & Railways	Sessions Book Trust 1992
Nock O.S.	Historic Railway Disasters	Ian Allen 1966
Percival D.	King's Cross Line Side 1958-1984	Ian Allen 1995
Pigram R.	The Hitchin Western Railway. Old Hitchin Life Vol 1 No 1	A Hitchin Historical Society Publication 1979
Talbot D.	Transcription of Hitchin South Signal Box Diary 1906-1968	Manuscript HItchin Museum
Townsend P.N.	Top Shed	Ian Allen 1989
Walker S.	Underground Hitchin	A Hitchin Historical Society Publication 2000
Wrottesley J.	The Great Northern Railway Vol. 1	Batsford,

Bedfordshire & Luton Archives & Records Service
First Garden City Heritage Museum, Letchworth
Hitchin Museum
Hertfordshire Archives & Local Studies
Letchworth Museum
National Railway Museum, York

http://web.ukonline.co.uk/cj.tolley/
http://www.winwaed.com

Ordnance Survey maps reproduced by kind permission of the Ordnance Survey, Southampton. Crown Copyright Reserved.

ABOUT THE HITCHIN HISTORICAL SOCIETY

Hitchin Historical Society, founded in 1977, currently has over 300 members. Besides arranging meetings and visits relating to Hitchin, Hertfordshire and local history in general, it encourages its members to undertake individual and group research on the history of their fascinating and historic market town.

INDEX

Italic numerals refer to illustrations;
Bold numerals refer to the start of a section.